C000212242

SPINNING IN A FAST WORLD

SPINNING
IN A FAST WORLD

JOHN EMBUREY

with Pat Gibson

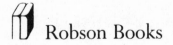 Robson Books

First published in Great Britain in 1989 by Robson Books Ltd,
Bolsover House, 5–6 Clipstone Street, London W1P 7EB

British Library Cataloguing in Publication Data

Emburey, John
    Spinning in a fast world.
    1. Cricket. Spin bowlers
    I. Title   II. Gibson, Pat
    796.35'822

ISBN 0 86051 540 0

Photoset by Rowland Phototypesetting Ltd,
Bury St Edmunds, Suffolk
Printed in Great Britain by St Edmundsbury Press Ltd,
Bury St Edmunds, Suffolk.

To Susie, Clare and Chloë with all my love

Contents

Preface

This book is not an autobiography nor is it a balanced account of England's more recent Test series. But I have used my experiences in the game – from bowling in the street in South-east London to captaining England against the West Indies – to write an unashamedly biased book about the often under-estimated and now endangered art of spin bowling. My object is to revive interest in spin bowling at all levels by encouraging youngsters to take it up, by giving cricket followers a better understanding of what it is all about and by convincing administrators that there is far more to the game than fast bowling.

Man with a Mission

NOTHING COULD HAVE been more ironic than my appointment as England captain against the West Indies in the summer of 1988.

There was I, the only spin bowler in the country still playing international cricket on a regular basis, being asked to lead England against the side that had done most to bring about this unfortunate state of affairs.

I did not have long to savour the experience. After just two Tests – and two defeats – at Lord's and Old Trafford, I was dropped for the next match at Headingley on the grounds that I no longer justified my place in the side on a pitch that has been loaded in favour of the seamers in recent years.

The selectors' decision was entirely understandable and I could have no complaints. After playing my part in England's successful defence of the Ashes in 1986–7, I had failed to take a single wicket in four home Tests against Pakistan the following summer. And though I felt I began to get my rhythm back in Pakistan that winter, and started the 1988 season with renewed confidence, I was still not taking enough wickets to support my contention that spinners still have a vital role to play in Test cricket.

As an off spinner myself, I am biased, of course. But I have become greatly concerned with the way cricket – and not just Test cricket – has gone in the Seventies and Eighties, with the West Indian fast bowlers ruling the world and even countries like India and Sri Lanka looking to seam rather than spin for their salvation, although India has started a revival. It is a sad situation for those of us who believe that there is more to the game than knocking batsmen's heads off.

Not that this was my biggest worry on the day I was summoned to Lord's and offered the job which must be the height of every English cricketer's ambition.

To get there, I had to run the gauntlet of an army of reporters and cameramen, most of whom were not the people I knew well from the Test and county circuit but an entirely different breed attracted by the scandalous – and, as far as I know, unfounded – allegations about Mike Gatting's social activities on the rest day in the first Test at Trent Bridge.

I felt desperately sorry for 'Gatt' but I suppose his dismissal was the inevitable outcome of a whole series of unfortunate events which were probably sparked off by the Test and County Cricket Board's refusal to replace umpire David Constant when the Pakistanis objected to him during their England tour. Certainly we seemed to be the victims of some well-orchestrated reprisals when we got out there, and in the end they provoked some unsavoury scenes.

The first, and in some ways, worst came in the first Test at Karachi where Chris Broad refused to leave the field after being given out caught behind. As England's vice-captain, I was on the tour committee responsible, among other things, for discipline, and I shared the general view that it was easy to sympathize with Chris because we had suffered a lot of questionable decisions, the game was slipping away and there was more disappointment and disbelief in his action than anything else. But I could also understand the feelings of many people back home who believed that he should have been disciplined.

Then came the incident that brought the second Test at Faisalabad to a standstill – Mike Gatting's infamous row with umpire Shakoor Rana. I cannot say much about what actually happened because I was off the field at the time, having treatment on my back, and did not see the confrontation 'live'.

But it certainly looked bad on television, with plenty of finger-wagging and facial expressions on both sides that carried a lot of venom. And again I could understand why people were unhappy about the repercussions, including that £1,000 'hardship bonus' from TCCB chairman Subba Row, which we did not really deserve.

With hindsight, admittedly, I now believe that if those two incidents had been dealt with properly at the time we might never have had the problems that followed in Australia, New Zealand and finally back home.

First, there was Broad again, smashing down his stumps in the Bicentennial Test at Sydney, an offence which I did not think was as serious as the one in Karachi but still demanded the £500 fine it incurred. Once more I'm sure it was a genuine case of disappointment and disbelief, this time with the position into which he had got himself, but I'm just as sure that any other batsman would have been delighted to score 139 on such an occasion. I certainly would have been.

Then we moved on to New Zealand where in the first Test at Christchurch Graham Dilley was fined £250 for swearing – though on this occasion I think he could consider himself a bit unlucky. There is nothing new in a player getting annoyed about what he considers to be a bad decision and swearing into the ground, which is what he did. The fact that his words not only echoed around a half-empty ground as well as being picked up by the television microphones was just unfortunate.

Finally we arrived at Trent Bridge for the first Test against the West Indies and those distasteful newspaper allegations which were to cost Mike Gatting the captaincy. I was offered the job and while I had every sympathy with 'Gatt' I had no qualms about accepting it. Life must go on and you just have to get on with it. And in any case it was something I had always wanted to do.

I thoroughly enjoyed the experience, too, even though I

only captained the side twice and we lost twice, which was obviously very disappointing.

We had gone into the series thinking that at last we had a chance of beating the West Indies after ten defeats in a row. Apart from Malcolm Marshall, their attack was raw and inexperienced, and we had beaten them in all three Texaco Trophy one-day internationals leading up to the Tests. We had a lot of good seamers, including Graham Dilley, Neil Foster, Gladstone Small, Paul Jarvis, Greg Thomas and Derek Pringle, as well as some very experienced batsmen in Graham Gooch, Chris Broad, Mike Gatting, David Gower and Allan Lamb. They had not got too many runs behind them in first-class cricket but that could be put down to the wickets, the weather and the preponderance of one-day games.

Unfortunately we could not get all of our best bowlers fit at the same time, but at least we stopped the run of defeats at Trent Bridge where Gooch and Broad in the first innings and Gooch and Gower in the second gave us a lot of encouragement. And, despite the sickening loss of Gatting, we went to Lord's with high hopes of doing well.

My first morning in charge could not have gone better. We took the first five West Indian wickets for 54 and I had only one nagging worry – that if our best bowler, Graham Dilley, could take five for 55, then their best bowler, Malcolm Marshall, could probably do even better, which he did with six for 32. And once we had been bowled out 43 behind everyone was filled with a familiar sense of foreboding.

I still thought we had a chance when we got five of them out in the second innings, but Gus Logie and Jeff Dujon put on 131 to put the game out of our reach. And even then I felt we should have saved it. Allan Lamb showed what could be done if we approached things in a positive frame of mind by playing a brilliant knock. But, sadly, the other main-line batsmen could not produce the goods and some indifferent batting cost us the match.

What disappointed me most was that we had lost on the best wicket we could have had for playing against the West Indies. It had pace and bounce with the ball coming on to the bat, making it conducive to stroke play. And I'm sure that is what we need to compete against the West Indies. Our batsmen would sooner see the ball coming through chest-high than bouncing unevenly, stopping or keeping low. That makes their job even tougher against bowlers of their pace.

Old Trafford could hardly have provided a greater contrast – so much so that Viv Richards alleged that the wicket had been soaked in the middle to take the sting out of his fast bowlers. But if you had seen the cracks in it before the match you would have known that it had not been 'doctored' at all. Anyway, as it happened, it didn't do as much as we hoped when we went into the match with two spinners, myself and John Childs, who was called up for his Test debut at the age of 36 after Nick Cook trod on a boundary rope and sprained his ankle when he wasn't even playing.

It looked as though it was going to help the spinners because of the cracks, but when it did turn it was very slow without much bounce. That is the difference between playing in England and playing in somewhere like Pakistan where the ball does bounce as well as turn. And I think the Lord's wicket would have done that, too, given another three or four days' play on it! That's another way we could compete against the West Indies. If wickets could be prepared earlier and kept dry for longer they would be bound eventually to help the spinners.

So we lost again at Old Trafford and while I don't really want to criticize our batsmen, it has to be said that they didn't play as well as we all know they can. They are, of course, very much governed by how well the bowlers bowl against them – and it must also be said that Malcolm Marshall was absolutely magnificent.

He did not bowl all that quickly but he used the conditions perfectly with a combination of swing and seam. It was

interesting to see how many of his wickets were either lbw or
bowled as a result of his pitching the ball up, because it meant
that the batsmen's inability to cope was purely a mental
problem. They all knew in the back of their minds that he had
bowled fast against them in the past and was still capable of
letting them have one short and quick; so they tended to be on
the back foot or only half forward, instead of getting well
forward like Gordon Greenidge and Desmond Haynes did
against our bowlers.

And what of the (temporary) captain? Well, as I said, I
thoroughly enjoyed the experience, I relished the thrill of
moving players around and manipulating them and, all things
considered, I don't think I did a bad job captaincy-wise. But at
the end of the day I have to admit that I could hardly expect to
stay in the side at Headingley where the selectors were never
going to pick more than one spinner in the squad and finished
up without even one in the side.

I had started the series well enough at Trent Bridge, getting
the wicket of Richie Richardson for the umpteenth time with a
ball that turned and bounced – but from that moment on I
knew that my place was going to be in jeopardy.

At home in 1980 and in the Caribbean in 1981 and 1986, I
had bowled well against the West Indies, and now they made it
perfectly plain that they were going to take a much more
positive and aggressive attitude towards me. Gordon Greenidge and Viv Richards had done that against me in the past but
suddenly Desmond Haynes, who had never tried it before, was
slogging me for a couple of boundaries and I conceded 95 runs
in 16 overs.

It was quite a compliment, I suppose, since they obviously
saw me as a threat and were trying to knock me out of the
attack. It was up to me to combat that policy by making sure
that I had my fielders in the right place and by bowling nega-
tively enough at the start to get on top of them before trying
any variation. And by giving me the captaincy in succession to

Bowling in tandem. Two spinners are better than one, and I consider myself very fortunate to have played for Middlesex and England at the same time as Phil Edmonds (below).

Two fellow off spinners for whom I have a great deal of sympathy. The extrovert Greg Matthews (left) keeps his cap on to bowl in a one-day international in Australia . . .

. . while Roger Harper is a study in concentration as he tries to make a point to the West Indian selectors.

Three old masters. Fred Titmus (above), all poise and balance, and Ray
Illingworth (below left), still getting his arm up high, bring their vast experience
to bear, while Derek Underwood (below right) shows that spin bowlers can be
aggressive too, as he puts every effort into his follow-through.

Contrasts in captaincy. Mike Brearley directs operations for Ian Botham with a deceptively casual air that hardly endeared him to Australian crowds (left)...

...but they were not too keen on Mike Gatting's British bulldog attitude either!

the unfortunate Mike Gatting, the selectors expressed their confidence in my ability to meet the challenge.

Unfortunately, I did not have that much confidence in myself. The 1987 season had been a major disappointment to me because I had taken only 35 wickets in first-class cricket and none at all in the Tests. It was mainly because I just wasn't bowling well enough, and the fact that I kept being selected to play for England was a sad reflection on the state of English cricket in that there was no other spinner with the all-round ability to make up for the lack of depth in the batting.

I do not consider myself as an all-rounder at Test level – I'm a useful number eight and a good number nine – but my batting has certainly been a bonus. It is unorthodox in that I don't really get behind the line of the ball but tend to back away to make room to play a kind of upper cut against the short ball and pull or sweep if the bowler follows me. Everyone has got to work out a way of scoring runs and that's the way I've done it.

There was a period of about 18 months when I was England's most consistent run-maker and I actually topped the batting averages in Pakistan with 207 runs at 69. And though my seven wickets cost 36 apiece I regained a lot of confidence in my bowling on wickets which really did give some encouragement to the spinner.

I got several wickets where I bowled batsmen 'through the gate' by opening them up and getting them to drive on the offside, which is what the off spinner is always aiming to do and quite the most satisfying way of getting somebody out. It was also nice to be used in an attacking role again instead of being asked to block up one end while the seamers take a rest, which happens all too often these days in Test cricket.

One of my major complaints in recent years has been that spinners are not used in the same positive way as are the faster bowlers. And I certainly believe that Phillippe Edmonds and myself, for example, could have made a far bigger contribution than we actually did by bowling in tandem to create opportunities not only for ourselves but for the other bowlers as well.

Sadly, Phillippe was no longer available in 1988, and while I desperately wanted to do well and take wickets, I went into the Test series feeling as though I needed to do a lot more bowling in county cricket to recapture my old rhythm and control. Once you get into a Test series there is precious little opportunity to do that, because with so many one-day games to fit in you sometimes do not get a bowl at first-class level between one Test and the next.

And so I dropped out of the England side with mixed feelings – intense disappointment that I had lost my two matches as captain but considerable relief that in my mission to conserve and promote the art of spin bowling I could at last get back to the basics . . . which is where I will take you now.

The Streetwise Spinner

LIKE SO MANY men with a mission – and, as I have said, mine is to conserve and promote the art of spin bowling – I was converted to the faith quite by accident. It happened when I was still very young, although when I first started to play cricket I was exactly the same as every kid of my age. I just wanted to bowl as fast as I possibly could.

We used to play in the back streets of Peckham in South London where I was born and grew up. The wicket was chalked on a wall and we would bowl from one side of the street to the other with a tennis ball. And the real skill in those games was to use the camber of the road – or, if you were really good, the kerb – to make the ball bounce steeply or fly off at different angles.

It did not seem to be any great feat at the time. But once I began to play the game more seriously it did not take me long to realize that what I had been doing was learning to bowl a good length and line. And that is still my greatest attribute to this day.

All I tried to do was run up and bowl at a brisk but very accurate medium pace; and at the level I was playing that was more than good enough to get me into the South London Schools Under-10 and Under-11 sides. I still have a cutting from a local newspaper relating how I had taken 18 wickets for 30 runs in one season – which is an average of 1.66 per wicket. I still find that quite incredible and only wish I could return similar figures now!

Yet my basic attitude has not changed at all. What I did then

– bowled straight, pitched the ball up and tried to hit the stumps – is, as far as I am concerned, what bowling is all about. And, to my mind, every young bowler should concentrate on no more than that.

I certainly had absolutely no intention of doing anything else . . . until one fateful day at Peckham Manor Secondary School when I was just 12 years old. There I was, bowling my medium-paced seamers, when suddenly, as if by magic, the ball turned almost at a right angle, leapt about three feet in the air, hit the batsman on the glove and ballooned up on the legside.

The teacher looked at me in astonishment and said: 'Do that again.'

I could only assume that somehow I had turned my wrist over while I was delivering the ball. So I tried to do the same thing again. Once more the ball turned and leapt at the batsman. And that was it. I have been bowling off spin ever since.

My 'conversion' was as accidental and uncomplicated as that. I never had any coaching as such. No one showed me how to grip the ball or taught me anything about 'loop' or 'drift' or any of the variations which I will explain later in this book. And when I was booked in for a couple of sessions at Alf Gover's famous cricket school at Wandsworth, the coach – not Alf himself, I hasten to add – did not even ask me to bowl. He just told me to put my pads on and have a bat, which was not the object of the exercise as far as I was concerned. I did not bother to go back a second time.

My dad – also named John – was not a cricketer and did not know a lot about the game. But he was very interested in sport and especially the fitness side of it, having been a bit of a boxer when he was in the Army. And he did his best to encourage me. He would take me to the matches when I played for the South London Schools sides and coughed up the money, which he could ill afford, to enable me to go on a London Schools tour to East Africa when I was 16.

Fortunately for me, there were two teachers at Peckham Manor, Mike Gunton and Des Soutter, who were very much involved in schools cricket. They took an interest in me and with their help and encouragement I went on to play for England Schools and Surrey Young Cricketers. By then other important cricket people – like the then Surrey coach Arthur McIntyre and captain Micky Stewart – were beginning to take notice. I remember Micky coming to watch us play at Mortlake, and after going on a Young Cricketers tour to Canada in 1970 I set my heart on playing for Surrey, my native county.

The following winter I attended the Surrey nets at Crystal Palace once a week and was looking forward to joining the staff when my hopes were dashed by a letter from Arthur McIntyre. It said that I obviously had a lot of ability and potential but money was tight and since they already had three good spin bowlers at the Oval they could not afford to give me a contract as well.

I could not argue too much about that. They had Pat Pocock, already an England off spinner, Intikhab Alam, the world-class Pakistan leg spinner, and Chris Waller, a talented left arm spinner who went on to play for Sussex. And with Pat only six years my senior and not even playing Test cricket at the time because Ray Illingworth was England's captain and off spinner, there were obviously not going to be many opportunities for me.

'Arthur Mac' suggested that I should approach Middlesex because Fred Titmus was a lot older than Pocock (nearly 14 years older, in fact) but I was a South London boy and was so bitterly disappointed with Surrey's decision that I did not even bother. It was Arthur himself – to whom I will always be grateful – who wrote to Middlesex on my behalf without my even knowing about it. That brought a letter from Don Bennett, the Middlesex coach, inviting me for a trial at Lord's. And though I was not aware of it at the time, my bowling in the nets brought a nod of approval from no less a judge than Titmus himself.

Coming from Surrey rather than Middlesex, I did not even know Fred then. And I did not get to know him that day, either. But he has since told me that Don Bennett asked him to have a look at me. Apparently he watched me bowl a few balls, then nodded his head and said: 'Yeah, he looks all right.' I must have had something.

That net was followed by a couple of 2nd XI games and an invitation to play until the end of the season – and that brought an abrupt end to my budding career as a financial clerk with the Amalgamated Union of Engineering Workers at Peckham, where I had worked since leaving school.

Professional cricket sounded much more glamorous but it did not seem to be such a big deal at the time, the summer of 1971. In fact I might not have left my desk if the AUEW had been prepared to give me time off to play cricket. But they would not. So I accepted Middlesex's offer of £600 for the remaining three months of the season – which was rather less than I had been earning with the union.

Nor did the life of a full-time cricketer turn out to be quite as glamorous as I had imagined. It had its moments – such as the thrill of claiming Kent's Bob Woolmer as my first victim in 2nd XI cricket, even though he had scored about 130 by the time I got him out. But soon I was face to face with the reality of the professional game. My first problem was trying to find a job during the winter, which is the biggest worry of all for any young cricketer. I have felt ever since that county clubs should make more of an effort and use their influence to fix their players up with alternative employment during the close season.

At least I had a new three-year contract to look forward to, and I could hardly wait to get back to Lord's and start plying the trade and honing the skills of an off spin bowler. Only it did not happen quite like that. Fred Titmus did not seem to take a great deal of notice of me and I felt that I was going backwards rather than improving as a bowler. Indeed between the ages of 18 and 22 I was convinced that I was stagnating and not making any progress at all.

Middlesex did not appear to share my view because they offered me a second three-year contract, but from my standpoint things didn't seem to be getting any better. There were the odd first team games (one in both 1973 and 1974, four in 1975 and 1976) but then it was back to the second team again. And in the end I became so frustrated that I considered giving up the game altogether. I was 20 years younger than Fred, but while I felt that I was rapidly getting older he seemed capable of going on for ever.

Looking back on it now, I realize that it was all part of the learning process. What had been happening during those early years, when I felt I was standing still, had been subtle changes in my action and my bowling generally. Each year my grip had altered slightly as I grew older and more experienced and tried to do different things with the ball. And all the knowledge I had gained playing for the 2nd XI during that seemingly interminable six-year apprenticeship made it a lot easier for me when finally I made the great breakthrough into the county side.

By a supreme irony, Fred had decided to join Surrey as their coach, and Don Bennett immediately came up to me and said my prospects would be much better in the future. So I stayed at Middlesex. I hardly need to tell you that I am glad that I did.

My first season (1977) was so successful that I finished up with 81 wickets from only 17 first-class matches, took five wickets or more in an innings nine times and was rewarded with my county cap. I didn't seem to be able to do anything wrong and although I still felt that I might have got into the side a year earlier, I did appreciate that by making me learn my trade and not rushing me into it Middlesex had given me the best grounding I could possibly have had.

It is so important for a spinner to have the respect of the

batsmen he is bowling against. And by the time I got into the first team a lot of the players I had faced in the 2nd XI had also got into their county sides. So already I had some sort of a reputation.

What I had to do then was maintain that reputation in county cricket and later, as things continued to go from strength to strength, in Test cricket – a totally different game from anything I had ever experienced before. It is played over five days rather than two or three, on better wickets, with different tactics and against far superior batsmen. But again you have to command their respect. And you can only do that by consistently putting the ball in the right place, not giving too many runs away and, of course, picking up a few wickets here and there.

Which is precisely what I was trying to do as a schoolboy in short pants at Peckham in the late Sixties. Whether you are trying to hit a kerb on a back street in South London or a patch of rough on a turning wicket at the Sydney Cricket Ground, there is simply no substitute for line and length.

That is the lesson I learned as a kid . . . and it is still paying dividends for me now.

Basics of Off Spin

HAVING ADMITTED THAT I never had any coaching as such, that I became an off spinner quite by accident and simply took it from there, I suppose it may seem presumptuous of me to try to tell other people how to bowl. But, in the hope of encouraging and helping cricketers, the young and the not so young, to take up spin bowling, I want to pass on what knowledge I have gleaned from nearly 25 years' experience at all levels of the game.

I have concentrated purely on off spin because off spin is what I know about – although the basic principles of the grip, the action and the way you release the ball to make it turn are just the same for the left arm spinner, only in reverse. Leg spin bowling, which has almost died out in England, certainly in the first-class game, because the wickets are so slow, is a different subject altogether and I will leave that to the specialists. What I do know is that finger spinners possess far more control than wrist spinners. And, as far as I am concerned, control is essential – especially in our conditions.

Before I get down to the mechanics of bowling off spin, it is important that the uninitiated should know what an off break actually is. It is a slow delivery that 'breaks' or turns from off to leg. And, apart from trying to deceive the batsman with the spin itself, the off spinner looks to confuse him with the length, direction and flight of the ball.

The off spinner is a multi-purpose bowler in that he can be used effectively on all kinds of wickets. He can bowl defensively on 'flat' pitches when the ball is not turning and try to lure the batsman into error; or he can attack when the conditions are more favourable. He is at his most dangerous when the ball is turning quickly, which is either when the wicket is very dry and starting to crumble or when it is wet and beginning to dry out. This latter condition is universally known as a 'sticky wicket'.

The grip. The first thing a spin bowler must be able to do, of course, is spin the ball. As I have said, my greatest strength as a bowler is my control of length and direction, which I developed through hours and hours of bowling seamers as a schoolboy. But it was the day I discovered that I could actually make the ball turn and bounce that was to shape my cricketing life. It happened as if by magic – yet once I was asked to do it again and worked out why it had been so different from all the balls I had bowled before, I realized that there was nothing mystical about it. All that had changed was the way I held the ball in my fingers and turned my wrist at the moment of delivery.

Whereas the seamer places his fingers on each side of the seam – albeit at different angles for different types of delivery – the off spinner grips the ball between the first and second fingers with the seam virtually at right angles to them. The ball should be held tightly between the top joints of those two fingers – you should be able to see a gap between the ball and the palm of your hand – with the other fingers and thumb being used only to support it. The further apart those first two fingers can be spaced in comfort, the greater their leverage on the ball and, therefore, the greater the degree of spin.

The action. Once you have learned how to grip the ball, the basic bowling action – side-on with the left arm high and the head looking over the left shoulder – is ideal for the off spinner. On delivery, the front leg is braced – in other words straight, with the head over the knee and toe – as the arm comes over to release the ball. As you let the ball go and follow through, the left arm comes straight down and back while the right arm continues across the body. The effect of this is that you actually pivot on your left foot and end up in a reverse position, with the right shoulder facing down the wicket and the left shoulder pointing behind you. That pivotal movement ensures that your bowling arm comes over the top or, at least, is as high as possible.

The release. At the start of the delivery, the wrist is cocked with the palm facing upwards. But as the ball is released, the first finger pushes hard against the seam and the wrist twists in a clockwise direction, as though you are locking a door, so that the side of the hand comes down vertically.

That is the basic method of off spin bowling and, in my opinion, all you need to know until you have developed a measure of control over your length and direction. Certainly, when I first started bowling off spin it was all I did know. I simply concentrated on bowling straight, keeping the ball up to the batsman, pitching it just outside the off stump and hoping that it would turn. All I was trying to do was bowl the batsmen out rather than get them caught – although obviously when you are very young and playing against boys of your own age you find that most of the time they are looking to hit you towards square leg or midwicket. That is why in schools cricket you should always have a deep square leg, a deep midwicket and perhaps a long on as well, because you are inevitably going to be slogged in that direction. When that happens, keep cool, pitch the ball right up . . . and hope that your fielders are confident enough to get under the catches without being frightened of damaging a finger!

Obviously the more the ball turns, the wider you need to bowl outside the off stump. It stands to reason that you do not want to be bowling so straight that the ball keeps turning harmlessly down the legside, missing the stumps altogether and giving the batsman a free hit. But, always remember, the more the ball turns, the fuller the length you should bowl, because you always want to keep the batsman on the front foot. If you pitch short, it gives him more time to watch the ball and makes it easier for him to score runs.

Variations. When you have mastered the 'stock ball' – or at least feel confident about bowling it accurately enough to gain the respect of the batsmen – then you can think about adding a bit of variety to your basic method.

The loop. 'Loop' is the word you most frequently hear when the 'experts' are passing instant judgement on a young spinner. Either he has got it, they will say, nodding in approval, or, shaking their heads sadly, he hasn't.

The fact is that there is nothing mysterious at all about loop. Indeed, it is the most natural thing in the world for the youngster just starting to bowl spin. You often see schoolboys, particularly when they are not very big, tossing the ball up and making it loop. All they are doing is getting it to rotate through the air before dipping in its flight and coming down quickly.

I can remember playing for Surrey Young Cricketers when I was in my teens and being told by my team-mate Stuart Surridge (son of the former captain . . . I'm not that old!) that I bowled with a nice loop. When I played against Stuart six years later, by which time I was a fairly seasoned professional, he observed that I had lost it and was bowling much flatter. A year or so ago I happened to play against him again and was delighted to hear him say that he thought my loop was coming back a bit – although it was still not quite as pronounced as it had been when I was 18.

It is my belief that the more cricket you play and the more experienced you become, the more you tend to lose your loop – and especially when you are as tall as I am and bowl 'downwards' anyway. Someone like Fred Titmus, who is much shorter, needed to throw the ball up into the air just to get it down to the other end. The most obvious exception to that general rule is Phillippe Edmonds who probably has the most natural action of any bowler in the game today. He has very strong fingers and does get the ball to arc through the air before dipping sharply. Perhaps my own loop will return as I get older and my bowling becomes slower.

The arm ball. Loop is essential for those spinners who do not turn the ball very much at any time – and there are plenty of them about. They have to rely on bowling slower and fuller, tempting the batsman down the wicket so that they can deceive him with flight rather than spin. But for someone like myself who tends to bowl much flatter, the most useful delivery (apart from the basic off break, of course) is the 'arm ball' or, as it is sometimes called, the 'drifter'. This is an off spinner in disguise, because the aim is not to make the ball turn but get it to drift or swing away in the air towards the slips.

Experienced spin bowlers have their own particular ways of doing things, but what I do for the arm ball is to place my first two fingers across the seam in the normal position for the off break and then just twist the ball so that one finger is in the orthodox seam bowling position, running down the length of the seam. As I come in to bowl, I cover up the grip with my left hand so that the batsman cannot actually see it. Then, as my arm comes over, instead of cocking the wrist and delivering the ball with the palm of my hand facing inside, I get my wrist behind the ball and simply push through as though I am bowling an away swinger.

The object with this delivery is to get the batsman to play inside the ball so that you either bowl him or get him caught at slip – or, if he chooses to sweep, trap him lbw.

The undercutter. Commonly called the quicker ball, because it is a faster version of the basic off break, the 'undercutter' skids rather than turns after pitching. It is bowled with an off break action, but instead of having your hand on top of the ball you keep your arm and wrist a little bit lower and bowl more around your front leg rather than over it. This makes the ball spin more horizontally towards the batsman, rotating from leg to off and pitching not on the seam but on the polished leather surface, with the result that it skids on.

I sometimes find myself undercutting the ball inadvertently because I am tired and my arm is getting lower, so that the ball drifts more but does not turn to the same degree. It is one of the problems of bowling for long spells with a high action, which does not necessarily give you tired fingers (the popular misconception) as much as an aching arm.

But whether you bowl the undercutter by accident or design, it is still a very handy weapon. By pitching it deliberately short, you can deceive the batsman into thinking that it is safe to pull across the line and pin him lbw when the ball does not bounce as high as he expects.

Using the crease. Some coaches talk about the 'top spinner' – which is spun forward towards the batsman so that it loops in the air before dropping a bit shorter than he expects – as part of the off spinner's repertoire, but I don't bowl it myself and do not really believe that it is necessary. My only other variations are concerned with using the crease to alter the length and trajectory of the ball. They involve only minor adjustments to the basic action but they all count at the end of the day.

Generally speaking, you will be bowling over the wicket and looking to pitch the ball on a full length just outside the off stump. But you can still vary your direction and flight by bowling one ball from close to the stumps and another from a foot or so wider – or simply by walking a yard and a half further back and coming in and bowling from a yard and a half behind where you would normally bowl. And when the ball is really turning you can bowl round the wicket to give yourself a much better chance of an lbw decision.

Whatever your variations, always remember one thing . . . that accuracy is of paramount importance. It is absolutely vital that you retain full control of your bowling to keep the pressure on the batsman. Use your variations sparingly so that he does not know what to expect, and don't attempt too much in case he gets on top of you.

Using the conditions. Although the spinner is at his best when the ball is turning sharply, either because the wicket is dry and crumbling or wet and drying, there are other types of conditions that he can equally exploit to his advantage.

Most wickets are a little bit 'green' to begin with, and although everyone expects the seamers to make the ball move around and do the early damage, it is a good idea to get the spinner on quickly and see what he can do. A green wicket means that there is some moisture in it, so that the ball grips on the turf when it hits the seam – and that will produce turn and bounce as well as seam and cut. I also think it is bad policy for captains not to use their spinners in order to put extra pressure on the first three batsmen, who get used to playing seam but do not normally see a lot of spin.

The best example of this was David Green, the former Lancashire and Gloucestershire opening batsman, who in 1965 became the only player ever to score 2,000 runs in a season without completing a century. When asked why he had never managed to get into three figures, he explained simply: 'I couldn't play the spinners. As soon as they came on, I was finished.'

As the match goes on and the wicket dries out and becomes easier for batting, you have to look to other elements to give you a little bit of assistance. And this is where the wind can come to your aid. Bowling into a headwind, you may find the ball dipping sharply in the air and making the batsman unsure of whether to play forward or back. But I find that a headwind can also upset my balance, and it is the cross breezes – especially those as strong as you get in places like Australia and the West Indies – which can be most helpful to the off spinner.

If you can get the ball to drift away with the wind and still put enough spin on it to make it turn back when it hits the seam, you can have the batsman in real trouble.

Whether he is coming forward or going back, the fact that the ball is drifting away will tend to draw the bat away from his pad and open him up so that if the ball does turn you have a good chance of bowling him through the 'gate'. This is the classic dismissal for the off spinner – something you are always hoping, and sometimes praying, to do.

It takes a few balls to get it right because you cannot tell how far the ball is going to drift, and thus do not know what line to start it on. And not every ball will drift to the same extent. That will also depend on the pace you bowl. The quicker the delivery, the straighter it will go; the slower you bowl it, the more chance it has of being taken by the breeze.

Obviously this is not the kind of thing you can do overnight. It demands good control and the ability to flight the ball – things that you have to work on throughout your career. And while you are concentrating on them, never forget the golden rules of spin bowling. You must pitch the ball up and try to get the batsman forward. The biggest crime is to bowl short and give him room and time to get on to the back foot.

Practice. It almost goes without saying that the best way for a spinner to practise is to get into the nets and bowl. But that is sometimes easier said than done. When I was at school I never practised at all – for the simple reason that there was nowhere for me to do so.

I did, however, have one piece of good fortune. There was a teacher at Peckham Park Primary School who would never let me bowl with a soft ball, not even in the playground with the other kids. I don't know whether he saw any potential in me at that age – I was only nine at the time and had not even started to bowl spin – but he insisted that I should be brought up with a hard ball. It didn't stop me playing with a tennis ball in the streets, and I'm not sure how much it helped overall. But, considering how far I have gone in the game, it seems to have had some kind of effect.

Almost all my early bowling was done in matches. My first club – Honor Oak at Dulwich Common in South-east London – did not have a colts section and at 16 I couldn't afford to travel to join the seniors at their twice-a-week practice sessions. So I was playing pretty regularly for my school in the mornings and my club in the afternoons. And when I got into representative cricket with London and England Schools, I could be playing up to four matches a week and hardly needed to practise anyway.

For most youngsters, though, practice is vital. Nowadays most clubs do have colts sections, regular nets and, usually, a senior player around to offer help and encouragement.

The major problem for the young spinner is to get the right kind of practice – which means the right kind of batsman to bowl at. If the batsman just wants to have a slog – as so many of them do – there is not much point in the spinner bowling at all. He needs to bowl against somebody who is going to treat him with a degree of respect, allow him to bowl properly and play each ball on its merits. Otherwise he is never going to learn how to bowl length and line.

But there are one or two things a spinner can do on his own, given the facilities and the necessary equipment. Fred Titmus, if he was not happy with the way he was bowling, would get back in the groove by picking up a couple of boxes of balls and going to the nets on his own. He would take out both the leg stump and the off stump, place them on a length just outside the line of the middle stump and try to bowl in between them. This was designed simply to get his line, his length and his rhythm without the distraction of a batsman thrashing around in front of him.

I did much the same kind of thing a few years ago when I felt I was not bowling particularly well during a match against Lancashire at Liverpool. I took a towel over to the net, laid it down on a length just outside off stump and bowled a few overs trying to pitch the ball on the towel. I had Don Bennett, the Middlesex coach, with me and after bowling line and length for a while I mixed it up a bit with slower balls and arm balls while Don checked where each one was landing.

Batting and fielding. Youngsters these days cannot rely solely on their spin bowling to reach the highest cricketing level. They must be able to bat and field as well.

Fred and I were lucky in that we could both bat a bit – rather more than a bit in Fred's case since he got more than 1,000 runs in a season seven times. I started off as a number eleven in second team cricket but gradually worked my way up the order until I had a season at number six for Middlesex. It was obviously too high for me – number seven or eight is more within my capabilities in county cricket – though I did have a good season, scoring more than 700 runs, including my first century, in 1983.

Fortunately, I have also been blessed with a strong arm and a safe pair of hands, whether at slip, gully or in the outfield – but, really, there is little excuse for any young cricketer being a bad fielder. Even if you cannot bat, you can improve your fielding; and that you can do on your own.

All you need to develop your throwing and catching is a brick wall. Throw a tennis ball against it, catch the rebound and throw again as quickly as possible. Or draw a set of stumps on the wall, throw the ball at them, field it and throw in again on the run, first in one direction and then the other. It is just a matter of hand to eye co-ordination. And, like everything else in cricket, hard work and dedication.

Physique. The last thing I want to do is put anybody off bowling spin, whatever their size and shape. But I do believe you have a big advantage if you are tall. I am not the world's greatest spinner of the ball and often have to rely on bounce as much as turn. That is why I find it very convenient to bowl overseas where the ball tends to get up higher than it does in England. And it stands to reason that it is easier to bang the ball into the ground and make it bounce when you are fairly tall.

The difference between a tall spinner and a short one is not dissimilar to the difference between quick bowlers such as Joel Garner and Neil Foster. 'Fozzy' himself is at least 6 ft 2 in tall and has a nice, high arm action. Yet Joel, being six inches higher with arms that seem to be about six feet longer, is so much more difficult for the batsman to pick up. What you think is a good length ball from Garner suddenly rears up under your chin, whereas a ball from Foster, pitching around the same spot, gets no higher than your waist and can be played with a degree of comfort. That is why Joel can be so lethal.

The extra height and arm length of a tall spinner enable him to deliver the ball from up to 18 inches higher than the smaller man. Therefore his length can vary by that amount.

It is much more difficult for somebody like Rajesh Maru, who is very short – around 5 ft 6 in compared with my 6 ft 2 in – to bowl a bit flatter and yet make it awkward for the batsman to pick up the length.

I well remember Rajesh joining Middlesex in 1979 and looking a good little bowler with a very nice loop. Indeed, I recall him playing for us against Essex at Southend and deceiving batsmen as good as Keith Fletcher and Kenny McEwan through the air. Yet in the nets, our batsmen – and especially a certain Mike Gatting – absolutely destroyed him. And the immediate reaction was: 'Oh, no, he can't bowl.'

That was totally wrong. Not only had he been mauled by one of the most destructive players of spin bowling in the world, but he had been given no proper chance, with the result that all his initial confidence was smashed out of him. Naturally he tried to bowl a lot flatter than before and as a result went to pieces completely. In the end he went off to Hampshire, where I was delighted to see that he got over his traumatic experience and is doing a good job for them.

It is a fact that most of the great spin bowlers of recent times – Jim Laker, Tony Lock, Lance Gibbs, David Allen, John Mortimore, Ray Illingworth, Bishen Bedi, Chandrasekhar, Ashley Mallett, Derek Underwood, Pat Pocock and Phil Edmonds – have all been fairly tall.

But there has been one notable exception. Fred Titmus

proved that the little fellows can make it to the very top. To do so, they have to maintain total control over their length and concentrate on trying to deceive the batsmen through the air. That demands practice, practice and more practice . . . and Fred was still visiting the nets regularly as he approached his 50th birthday!

Learning the Trade

ONE THING A spinner or, come to that, any cricketer, must never forget is that there is no end to the learning process. So now that I have told you how to bowl off spin – or, at any rate, how I bowl off spin – let me say something about the things I have learned during my progress through the various levels of the game into Test cricket and how I endeavour to cope with different situations.

When I first come on to bowl – and this applies wherever and whenever I bowl, whether it is at Lord's or Lahore, in a one-day game or a Test match – I try to get on top of the batsman straightaway, forcing him on to the defensive and giving him nothing to hit at all. That means bowling three or four very accurate overs of basic off spin, not too flat but certainly without too much air. Only when I have established a measure of control over him will I think about introducing any variations or making a few experiments.

Those first three or four overs should tell you all you need to know about the pace and bounce of the wicket – and whether the ball is turning or not. They might even indicate that you ought not to be bowling at all! But if you and, more importantly, the captain have already seen one or two balls turn and bounce a little, then all well and good. You will naturally be looking to bowl that delivery most of the time.

Unless you are very lucky, however, the chances are that the wicket will not be taking much turn at all. In that case, the most important thing to be considered is the bounce, because that will determine the length you can bowl. This can vary by as much as three or four feet depending on how high the ball bounces. If it is a really bouncy wicket, you can get away with bowling that much shorter, since the ball will hurry on to the batsman and tuck him up.

But on flatter wickets, where the bounce is not so steep, you cannot afford to pitch short because all you are doing is giving the batsman time to get back and hit you on both sides of the wicket, either cutting through the offside or pulling past midwicket. Basically, then, the slower the wicket, the more difficult it is to find the right length – and the more important it is to pitch the ball up. Better too full than too short.

Once you have settled on the length you are going to bowl, you can start to vary it a bit, giving the odd ball a little more air, dropping one just a fraction shorter or slipping in the occasional arm ball to see if you can get any swing. If none of these variations proves successful, it is back to concentrating on your line and length, always trying to get the batsmen to drive, always hoping that the ball will turn – and always exercising the greatest quality any spin bowler can possess. That, without a shadow of doubt, is patience.

It is a fact of cricket life that a fast bowler does not have to use any psychology at all. He is just looking to blast the batsman out. And if he gets hit for four he will simply respond by trying to knock the batsman's head off. For the spinner it is much more of a battle of wits. If he gets hit for four or six – and it is much easier to slog a spinner than it is to slog a fast bowler – he has to accept it as part and parcel of the game and just get on with the job.

As a spinner, you have to realize that batsmen *are* going to get after you sometimes, they *are* going to hit you over the top, they *are* going to smash you for fours and sixes. You may still be bowling the right line and length but you must grin and bear it. If I bowl a bad ball, I have only myself to blame. If the batsman plays a particularly good shot, I will give him some credit for that. And even if it is a downright slog, a mishit or an edge that somehow finds its way to the boundary, I can say to myself: 'Well, fair enough, he hasn't played a very good shot but that's the way it goes.'

My reaction to that kind of treatment is to be as mean as I possibly can be in my bowling and try to recoup my losses. Fred Titmus taught me that bowlers do not bowl to give batsmen runs. He had taken nearly 3,000 first-class wickets but he always insisted:

'If they want runs off me, they'll have to bloody well score 'em . . . and the more times they try to score the more chance I have of picking up a wicket.'

Fred had the patience to wear the batsmen down. And that is a lesson I have never forgotten. The only time I do lose patience – in fact I tend to go berserk! – is when someone pinches a sneaky single or turns a one into two or a two into three through a bad piece of fielding. That can be very frustrating.

Yet there is ample compensation and intense satisfaction for the spinner when everything does go right. It is not very often, believe me, that you find yourself in perfect control of your line and length, with the bounce there and the ball turning enough to find the edges and sometimes beat the bat altogether. But that is what happened to me against Kent at Dartford in 1983 when I took six of the first seven wickets for only 13 runs and was very disappointed not to get at least two of the last three wickets as well.

That remains the best bowling spell of my career although there have been a few other occasions when everything just seemed to fall into place. It happened once or twice in South Africa. It happened in Sri Lanka when I took six for 33 in the inaugural Test in Colombo. And it happened in the first Test against Australia at Brisbane in 1986 when everything clicked in the second innings. The batsmen were looking to dominate me but I picked up both Dean Jones and Allan Border and kept up the pressure to take three wickets for two runs the next morning.

Unfortunately you cannot bowl like that all the time. As a rule things do not go quite so smoothly. Then you have to take each batsman as he comes and work on him individually – which can be difficult when you see someone like Mike Gatting or Graham Gooch, Allan Border or Viv Richards coming to the crease.

Take 'Gatt' for example. Fortunately I do not have to bowl against him but if I did I would be only too well aware that he is a batsman who just loves to get back and cut the off spinner. So I would be looking to deny him the room to get back and cut me by bowling a full length and perhaps undercutting the ball to make it go straight rather than turn. That way he wouldn't be able to cut and might be tempted to sweep – another shot he favours – and if I were bowling wicket to wicket I would have a good chance of getting him out lbw.

It can take years and years of experience for a spinner to compete on equal terms against batsmen with so much natural ability and aggressive intent. And you only get that experience by bowling against the best players, probing for their weaknesses and, when you think you have found one, working out ways to exploit it. Because of this, spinners tend to come of age in their early 30s, reaching a peak around 33 and then levelling off for a while before going into a gradual decline.

Spinners stay at the top longer than quicker bowlers not only because they obviously take less out of themselves over the years but also because they get better with age. Their arms may be lower and their waistlines thicker, and they may not be quite as athletic around the field. But all the experience they have gained, all that knowledge they have stored up, tells them where to bowl the ball in every given situation.

It is almost as though the wheel has gone full circle. They have lost some of the pace and strength that they once had and thus bowl much slower, giving the ball more air and getting back to the very basics of spin bowling. They are using their heads as much as their arms and fingers to get batsmen out.

This is why cricketers like Fred Titmus and Ray Illingworth were able to carry on playing into their fifties, why Norman Gifford and Derek Underwood were still going strong in their forties . . . and why I like to think that I have a few more good years left in me yet.

I could hardly believe my eyes when Fred came back to play for Middlesex in 1982 – when he was 49! I would be standing at mid on or mid off and watching open-mouthed as he tossed the ball up in the air and just seemed to leave it hanging there. I had never seen batsmen groping so far forward in their efforts to reach the ball as the Surrey players were on one particularly memorable occasion. It was as though the ball was never going to arrive. And I could not help thinking that there I was, already a fully-fledged Test bowler, still learning from the little maestro.

Fred had always given me tips in the few games we played together for Middlesex. If a new batsman came in who I had not seen before he would give me a quick run-down on the way he played, whether he liked to get on to the front foot or the back foot, whether he would just be looking to play me or trying to hit me over the top, that sort of thing.

Yet it was not so much what he told me as what he showed me by example that was the most vital part of my cricket education. I am sure that the best way to learn, the way that many top players develop in the game, is by being in the same side as a master craftsman such as Fred. I learned most of my bowling simply by watching Fred – and Phillippe Edmonds as well – bowling for Middlesex. And you have only got to look at the technique of players like Martyn Moxon and Bill Athey to realize how much they learned from batting with Geoff Boycott for Yorkshire. You can see Boycott in the way they play, especially Billy who is pure 'Boycs' with his defensive shots and straight bat; and that has come about entirely through watching a technically great player at the other end.

Not many people are fortunate enough to have the benefit of

this kind of personal experience, but everyone can learn from watching the leading players in action. And the marvellous thing nowadays is that with video recorders available they can make tapes of the big matches and study the players' techniques in even greater detail.

So if you really want to concentrate on spin bowling, make yourself a tape of a particular spinner at his work. Then watch it ball by ball, over by over, and try to figure out what the bowler is trying to do, why he is always putting the ball in a certain place or why he has suddenly decided to vary it.

You may see six balls from an off spinner pitching just outside the off stump which all look exactly the same . . . but one might get hit through the offside because it is a shade wider or a fraction shorter, another might be flicked through mid-wicket because it is too straight and too full, and another might curve in the air that little bit more and beat the outside edge.

Look for the bowler's reaction when somebody tries to get after him and at what stage he changes his plan and attempts something different to contain the batsman. And if the bowler gets someone out, try to analyse how and why it happened.

Try, as a result, to emulate the professionals and store up your own little bits of knowledge when you actually play the game yourself. At school, make a mental note of the kids who have scored runs against you and where they have hit you. At club level, work out the opposition batsmen, anticipate how they are going to play and bowl accordingly the next time you meet.

The obvious difficulty as you progress from one level of the game to the next is that the standard becomes that much higher, you get less margin for error and, with more attacking fields, you have to bowl fewer bad balls. It puts you under much more pressure and, in my experience, changes you as a bowler. For better or worse . . .

The Modern Way

I HAVE TO admit that I was a much more natural and gifted off spinner before I became a full-time professional cricketer. And in some ways I regret that my bowling had to change. But I had no choice in the matter. What happened to me was simply a reflection of the way the game has evolved from the days of the amateurs and the professionals, the gentlemen and the players, into a much more practical, hard-headed pursuit of success.

It was former Middlesex and England captain Mike Brearley who, more than anyone, bridged the gap between amateurism and professionalism – and it was 'Brears' who threw me in at the deep end when I first got into the county side in the early Seventies.

I had already discovered that there was a vast difference between bowling in club cricket and bowling in 2nd XI cricket, but that gulf seemed almost insignificant once I started playing for the first team. I had been used to bowling the old-fashioned way with basically defensive fields and only one close fielder at short leg. Brearley insisted on putting a man in at silly mid off as well as forward short leg. That immediately made me into a different type of bowler altogether.

Instead of bowling my 'natural' line to a full length just outside the off stump in an attempt to get the batsman driving and induce those little inside edges that go off bat and pad to short leg, I had to tighten up my line considerably. With those two fielders there, the bowler's view down the wicket is very narrow indeed and you don't want to endanger their limbs or even their lives by giving the batsman the chance to drive on either side of the wicket with them in the firing line. So I had to give the ball much less width and direct my attack much more towards the stumps – in simple terms, bowl straighter.

At the start I seemed to be under rather more pressure than the batsmen. I was nervous and bowled a few bad balls. Fortunately, though, I had an outstanding captain who knew exactly what he was doing and what he wanted his players to do.

Brearley talked to me, explained the field placings – in fact they were pretty orthodox really, with that one notable exception – and instilled in me a philosophy of bowling that has formed the basis of the way I have bowled ever since. It may have developed because of the way the Australian batsmen played Jim Laker way back in 1956 when he took those 19 wickets at Old Trafford. But by the early Seventies Brearley had introduced that silly mid off position at Middlesex simply because batsmen were playing more with their pads, i.e. with their bats behind their pads.

With the bat behind the pad there were fewer inside edges to leg slip and many more balls going via the pad and then the bat out on the offside. So nowadays silly mid off exerts more pressure on batsmen than leg slip, which is something of a luxury.

This is an aspect of off spin bowling that has changed enormously over the years – and I am sure that Fred Titmus and his generation do not approve. Fred himself never liked that man up on the offside. He much preferred to bowl without too many fielders around the bat, close the gaps elsewhere and challenge the batsmen to try to hit the ball through the field or, failing that, over the top. That romantic notion has virtually disappeared in the game's evolution. Today the emphasis is very much more on attack.

As I have said, I am not altogether happy with the modern methods myself, and sometimes think that we are losing sight of what off spinners really should be doing. And with the one-day game forcing you to bowl a similar, flatter line, more towards leg stump so that you are only being hit on one side of the wicket, I admit that I could have got into a bit of a rut.

But as the late Jim Laker, unquestionably the greatest off spinner in the history of the game, wrote in his book *Cricket Contrasts* (Stanley Paul): 'I have given it (the one-day game) a lot of thought and have come to the conclusion that I would have had to cope in the same way as people like Emburey have done by increasing their pace and bowling a fuller length at middle stump or middle and leg.'

All you can do is try to be flexible; and there are times when I do give the ball more air and get back to bowling more like I did when I first started. It certainly happens overseas where the wickets tend to have rather more pace and bounce than they do in England and there is no need to bowl quite as flat or push the ball through as quickly.

I also bowl with more loop against left handers – for a purely personal reason. Bowling to right handers, I get very frustrated if I am continually beating the bat only for the ball to keep cannoning into the pads. Because of that I push the ball through flatter and try to beat the bat on the outside rather than between bat and pad. I find it much more rewarding when you can actually see the batsman groping for the ball as it turns away from him. So against left handers I give it a great deal more air. It looks better, the crowd enjoys it and you get a far greater sense of satisfaction from knowing that you have actually beaten the batsman. With the right hander you can never be quite sure whether you have beaten him – or whether he has just kicked the ball away.

Nevertheless, there are those occasions when you really do have to get back to bowling the way spinners are traditionally supposed to bowl . . . when the pitch is absolutely flat, there is no bounce, the ball is not turning and wickets are desperately hard to come by. Then you have to revert to a defensive role and try to put the onus on the batsman to come after you.

You can do that by putting him under pressure – not by having fielders on top of him but by getting the crowd on his back instead! The spectators know that cricket, and especially Test cricket, can be slow at times but they dislike seeing a batsman getting completely bogged down. So you don't risk your variations in case you give him something to hit. You just keep coming up with stock ball, stock ball, stock ball, knowing that he cannot get it through your infield, and then toss up a slower one in the hope that the pressure has got to him and he will take a chance by trying to hit it over the top.

That is the way spinners used to bowl in the old days, a lot slower and with much more air. The big difference, however, was that the batsmen were actually prepared to advance down the wicket and have a go at lofting the ball over long on and long off, even though there were fielders back on the boundary waiting for them to do just that.

You don't see too much of that kind of thing now. The game has changed in that batsmen all the way down the order value their wickets more highly. I used to think that nothing illustrated better the difference between the attitudes of the amateurs and the professionals than the intense north–south rivalry you found in the County Championship. The northern batsmen put the accent far more on defence and you really had to bowl them out whereas the southerners were prepared to be more aggressive and adventurous, go for their shots and take a few chances.

That general mentality still exists to a certain extent. In the north they seem resolved to save the game rather than determined to win it. In the south they think of winning from the outset and only settle for a draw if they are not in a position to win. Yet individual batsmen everywhere seem to have hardened their attitudes, and spinners do not find so many easy pickings.

So you have to bowl to your strengths. Mine, for the various reasons I have already stated, are accuracy and control, line and length, and the ability to put batsmen under pressure. I get a fair amount of criticism at times (most significantly from ex-England players now working for the media) on the grounds that when I do get hit over the top I bowl even flatter than usual. But, to my mind, that is absolute nonsense.

There are flighty bowlers around who will always have a couple of men back on the boundary; but that is not for me. I can be flexible but I prefer to have men around the bat, and in that situation there is not much point in encouraging the batsman to hit you over the top because there is no one there to take the catch.

When I am hit, the usual reason is that I have varied my bowling when in control and suddenly given the batsman the chance to dominate me. Of course it is nice to have a couple of men out in the deep to give you the option of bowling a little slower with a bit more air – but the trouble with the modern trend is that it is very difficult to have an 'in-and-out' type of field. Most of the time you will just have an 'in' field; and that is the basic reason why spinners do not bowl slower and toss the ball up more.

With attacking fielders at silly mid off, short leg and slip, and others filling the gaps to save the singles, you just do not have enough men to patrol deep square leg, deep midwicket or long on, which is where batsmen will hit you if you give them the chance. So you simply cannot afford to bowl with as many variations as you might like.

I am not saying that this is the way you have to bowl at school or club level. Indeed, the standard of spin bowling, the quality of batsmanship and the unorthodox shots that are played would make it downright dangerous for the close fielders. It is dangerous enough at the highest level but the professionals must accept the risks involved because we are being paid to do a job and we have to produce the goods.

That, at any rate, is the modern philosophy . . . and I regret that I have been affected by it, and may even have suffered from it, as much as anybody.

The three grips that I use for bowling off spin and its variations, the arm ball and the undercutter, as the batsman sees them.

A (top left) is the basic off break, my stock ball. The ball is gripped between the first and second fingers. The index finger is across the seam with the second finger underneath and the top knuckle pressed against it. The wrist is cocked just before delivery to impart the spin.

B (top right) is the arm ball. The index finger is placed along the seam with the hand behind the ball rather than alongside it to push through on delivery.

C (left) is the undercutter, with the index finger back across the seam but the hand again behind the ball as in the arm ball. On delivery, the index finger pushes through to make the ball pitch on its polished leather surface rather than the seam and skid on towards the slips.

 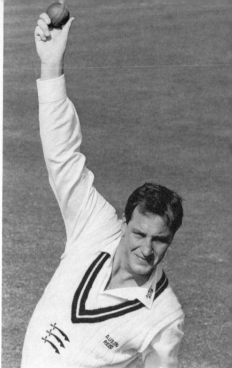

The batsman's view of the three deliveries.

A (top left) basic off break,
B (top right) arm ball,
C (left) undercutter

The same three deliveries seen from behind the bowler's arm.

A (top left) basic off break (note hand alongside the ball and the arm high)
B (top right) arm ball (note index finger along the seam and the hand behind the ball)
C (right) undercutter (note index finger across the seam, ready to push through)

The follow-through.

A (left) is for the basic off break. The left arm has gone back while the right arm continues down across the body and past the right knee, completing a pivotal movement which leaves you with the right shoulder facing down the wicket and the left shoulder pointing behind you.

B (right) is for the arm ball and the undercutter. Instead of continuing straight down, the right arm goes more around the body to make the ball go towards the slips.

In the Captain's Hands

IN MY EXPERIENCE of schools, youth, club, county and Test cricket, the fate of the spin bowler is in the hands of one man – the captain. If he is sympathetic towards what you are trying to achieve, you have every chance of success; if he is apathetic, you have no chance at all. And, more often than not, the captain's attitude depends on how he himself looks to play spin bowling.

Not all captains, of course, are batsmen; but the vast majority are. And there could be no better illustration of what I am talking about than the contrast between the two captains I have played under for Middlesex – Mike Brearley and Mike Gatting.

Brearley had a high regard for spin bowlers. He was not the kind of batsman who just went in and tried to smash them around the ground – or out of the ground, if possible. He relished the challenge of pitting his wits against a good spinner, finding it much more of an intellectual challenge than attempting to survive the sheer physical bombardment of the fast bowlers.

Gatting is different. As a batsman he has no regard for spin bowlers at all – or at least not when he first took over the captaincy from Brearley. He didn't even think they should be allowed to bowl, so he just tried to bludgeon them out of the attack as soon as they came on. Admittedly he did this with a remarkable degree of success, and I was thankful to have been playing on the same side!

When he started to captain Middlesex he was very doubtful

whether he wanted both Phillippe Edmonds and myself in his side, even though we were considered to be two of the best spinners in the game. Nor was he ever sure whether to bowl us or not when a batsman came in and tried to dominate in the same way that he does.

Fortunately for us, he soon came to appreciate that we were good bowlers and that his opinion might have been clouded by the fact that just as we did not have to bowl against him he did not have to bat against us. But the clash between a younger captain and two older spinners did tend to cause a little bit of friction in the dressing room.

Field placing was an obvious area for disagreement. Whereas Brearley, the methodical, analytical batsman, would set a more or less orthodox field for the spinner (with the exception of that man at silly mid off), Gatting, the bustling, bristling strokemaker, wanted the fielders placed where he was in the habit of smashing the ball. And that brought us into immediate conflict.

For the off spinner, 'Gatt' always wants a man square on the offside because that is where he likes to pummel the ball away. But I don't want that man there. I prefer to have him at extra cover.

My reasoning is simple enough. If I need a man square on the offside, it means that I am bowling too short and giving the batsman room to get on to the back foot and hit me there – which is not my aim. Therefore, I try to get the batsman on to the front foot looking to drive. The problem is that in the absence of an extra cover, there is no encouragement for me to pitch the ball up, because of the risk of giving away too many runs. So in the end I finish up bowling a foot shorter than I normally would, and the ball is hit square on the offside.

I never used to get cut. Never ever. But now I do. And it is purely because of the change in captaincy, purely because of the vast difference in the way that Brearley played spin bowling and the way that Gatting plays it.

The only solution to the dilemma is a degree of flexibility on both sides, a compromise depending on the state of the game, the condition of the wicket and the way the batsman is playing. But it is the kind of situation that is always likely to be tricky when any new, young captain takes over a side containing two older, more experienced and pretty forthright characters who are specialists in what they do. Naturally enough, the captain wants to do things his way but he may not have the same depth of knowledge as some of the people under him. In such circumstances, I believe he is better off using their knowledge, accepting what they are trying to do and letting them set their own fields.

Of course, that is a fairly extreme example of what can happen, and I have to admit that there are a lot of bowlers around who do not actually know what they are trying to do and will automatically look to the captain, whoever he is, to do the tactical side of the job for them.

Yet I do feel that it is always in the bowler's interests to give a great deal of thought to the way he approaches every given situation – and always in the captain's interests to listen to him. After all, it is the bowler who is trying to take the wickets.

It is fair to say that the more experience a captain possesses, the more understanding he has of the spin bowler's art and craft. And it may well be that the lack of captaincy experience has contributed to England's frequent inability to bowl sides out in recent years. Mike Brearley certainly understood the importance of having a balanced attack – and so did Keith Fletcher, another captain with the utmost respect for spin bowling. But Ian Botham, Bob Willis, David Gower and, most recently, Mike Gatting have not necessarily shared their views.

Willis, for all his years in the game, was still a relatively inexperienced captain when he got the job – and, not surprisingly after taking 325 wickets himself, he was adamant that fast bowlers won Test matches. You only had to look at the way he handled Dilip Doshi, the Indian Test left armer who played

for Warwickshire, to know what big Bob thought about
spinners. He would just put Dilip on at one end and leave him
bowling away for over after over on the flattest pitch, regard-
less of whether he was being slogged out of sight or not.

Botham had a similar attitude. We all know his views on
spin bowling, too, from the way he looks to play it. He liked to
put his spinners on when there was not much else happening so
that they could get the overs out of the way and hasten the
arrival of the next new ball.

It was much more enjoyable playing under Gower because
he was far more flexible and prepared to listen to what we had
to say. I think he appreciated that we knew more about what
we were trying to do than he did and therefore he used
Phillippe and myself as we wanted to be used. He let us set our
own fields – as long as we went through him to do it, obviously
– and because of that he gained a lot of respect from both of us.

It paid off for him against Australia in 1985. Although we did
not take an awful lot of wickets, we did put the batsmen under
pressure in most of the matches, and helped England into
winning positions.

That was a classic example of how to use experienced
spinners, accustomed to bowling long spells, to dictate the
course of Test matches by keeping things tight and picking up
the odd wicket until the new ball is due, and then coming back
after the anticipated breakthrough to chip in again.

Those tactics worked well throughout that summer and –
though I was not there myself because of my ban for going to
South Africa – I imagine they had also worked well for David
the previous winter when Pat Pocock partnered Phillippe on
the successful tour of India. Knowing Pat as well as I know Phil,
I am sure they both had plenty to say; and having sold
themselves to David, they delivered the goods by bowling
England to victory in the crucial second Test in Delhi and
finishing up with 27 wickets between them in the series.

Which brings me back to Mike Gatting, who may feel that

his erstwhile vice-captain has been a little bit severe on him so far! He had a desperately difficult job in taking over from David Gower during that depressing, even distressing period when England were being 'whitewashed' in the West Indies and then losing successive home series against India and New Zealand. But it all began to come right for him in Australia.

Luckily for 'Gatt', everything tended to go our way from the moment we played well and Australia played badly in the first test at Brisbane, and we were never under too much pressure for the rest of the series. Everyone was full of confidence and doing the jobs they were supposed to do, which made his position a lot easier.

It meant that he was able to captain the side in the way he wanted – and that was basically to do his own thing and create his own character as the England skipper. All the players respected him for that, and as the tour went from success to success it increased his strength and credibility. He also learned a lot, including, I am happy to say, a greater understanding of how to use the spinners. Essentially, I think he matured and could only get better.

That impression was confirmed when we went to Pakistan in 1987–8 and came across quite a few wickets that were hard and dry and totally devoid of grass, naturally helping the spinners. 'Gatt', still very much a seam-orientated captain, quickly realized that there was nothing in them for the quicker bowlers, so the spinners really came into their own.

A captain can only benefit from using spinners and getting involved with them and, as a result, I think that as he learned more about our views of the game, his confidence in handling us increased. So it was even more sad that what happened on that tour should have tarnished his image as England captain and eventually led to his sacking in the summer of 1988.

That gave me the chance to lead the side – albeit briefly – and my biggest thrill came at Old Trafford when I made up my mind to open the bowling in the West Indies' first innings after they had bowled us out for 135. When Mike Brearley was captaining Middlesex, he would sometimes open with two spinners if he thought the wicket might turn, and I don't think it's a bad idea to get them on early when the ball is new and hard and create a little bit of pressure that the opening batsmen are not accustomed to. My senior advisers – Graham Gooch as vice-captain, Gatting and Gower – were not too sure about it but I went ahead all the same and was almost rewarded with a wicket.

I don't think that would have happened if anybody else had been captain – though it would have been interesting to see if Chris Cowdrey, an adventurous captain if ever there was one, had tried something similar in the same kind of circumstances.

In my view, Cowdrey was the best selection to take over from me for the last two Tests against the West Indies because another Indian tour was looming the following winter and he had had the experience of going there on Gower's tour.

I was not convinced about either of the other two main contenders, Kim Barnett and Mark Nicholas. I doubted whether they were good enough batsmen against bowling of the highest class or good enough captains to compete successfully at Test level. Neither of them had won anything until the 1988 Benson and Hedges Cup Final when Hampshire beat Derbyshire, and whereas I was delighted that Hampshire had finally made the breakthrough without their overseas stars, Gordon Greenidge and Malcolm Marshall, Nicholas really should have won something before then. As for Barnett, I felt his captaincy lacked variety, which was hardly surprising since Derbyshire invariably fielded a side containing five seamers.

In Cowdrey's favour was the fact that he was in the process of leading Kent to within one point of the County Championship, which was a remarkable achievement considering that he had a side without any real stars. Kent's overseas player, Roy Pienaar, was obviously a batsman of quality but Cowdrey himself was the inspiration, scoring runs, taking wickets and, through his own example, turning them into an exceptional fielding side. He is a captain who is always prepared to try something different and I wished him every success. My only reservation, having lost the job through my own performances as a player, was that sooner or later he would have to be judged on his.

Unfortunately for Chris, that judgement came far sooner than anyone expected. Injury forced him out after just one, predictably unsuccessful, Test at Headingley and the selectors turned instead to my great friend, Graham Gooch, whose performances throughout the summer had been quite outstanding and made him the one player whose position in the side could not be questioned. Political ramifications apart – and I don't think they should come into it anyway – Graham's appointment was perfectly logical for purely cricketing reasons. He had given up the Essex captaincy in 1987 because he felt it was affecting his batting; but in 1986, the year he took over from Keith Fletcher, he had done a magnificent job in leading them to the County Championship. Once he had reasserted himself as a world-class batsman in the MCC Bicentenary match at Lord's, he just went from strength to strength. In my opinion, that made him the obvious choice to lead England until they could find a younger captain good enough to hold his place – or, alternatively, revert to Mike Gatting.

Yet I could not help wondering whether the changes in captaincy would ever make any difference to England's results . . . and whether the time had come to introduce a revolutionary new method of team selection involving just the team manager and the captain, rather than a selection committee under a chairman with the authority to override their point of view.

During my brief term as captain, Bill Athey rang me up out of the blue and said: 'I don't know whether you've had a meeting yet but have you talked about David Lawrence of

Gloucester? He's still quick but he's reduced his run, he's got a much better line and he's bowling really well. Most of the batsmen we've come across this season have had problems against him – even the West Indies.'

Now I don't know whether this sort of thing has happened before but I'm sure it's the kind of attitude we have to develop around the counties. Players like Athey should be encouraged to inform the manager or the captain about who is playing well so that they actually pick players who are in form instead of players who might have been in form four or five weeks earlier.

This could be the basis for a new selection process co-ordinated by the manager and involving a network of county captains, senior players, managers, coaches and even umpires who are around the county circuit all the time. Then if things do go wrong, the critics would know who to blame. When I was captain, I thought that team manager Micky Stewart received a lot of unfair criticism because he was only one of five selectors and should not have been left to make excuses when the side did badly.

In my experience, the captain does usually go into a Test match with the side he wants, and once on the field that side is in his hands. But I do feel that there needs to be a change in the system of selection.

The Spinner's Nightmare

THE BEST PLAYERS of spin bowling in England fall into three distinct categories: the older, vastly experienced batsmen who grew up in an age when spinners seem to have been much more highly respected than they are now; the modern, more aggressive strokemakers who developed methods to meet the demands of a game that was changing with the influx of one-day cricket; and the young ones who do not give a stuff for tradition or reputation but simply respond to the needs of the moment.

It will surprise no one when I name Geoff Boycott as the best English batsman, from a technical point of view, I have ever bowled against – but I doubt whether many people could guess which two players I have most dreaded bowling against in the past few years.

I will conceal their identities for a while, for I must start with the man who has dominated every discussion about the state of English batsmanship throughout my career, not just because of his own legendary individual performances but also because of the effect he has had on the players around him. Everything you ever hear about Geoffrey Boycott seems to be a contradiction in terms – and the way he played spin bowling is no exception.

Technically, his batting against spin – or any other type of bowling, come to that – was an object lesson. Every aspect of it was right. His feet were in the correct position all the time. He did not push at the ball but let it come on to the bat, which is one of the most important things a batsman has to do against spin. And he had the patience to wait for the loose ball, either slightly overpitched or just a fraction short of a length, before invariably putting it away to the boundary. And yet . . .

Yes, I am afraid there is always a qualification whenever anyone talks about Boycott. For all his greatness as a batsman, he was one player against whom the spinner could always enjoy bowling. That was because you knew that he was never going to look to dominate you or try to take you apart. He was quite happy to allow the spinner to bowl, so it was always possible to develop a good line and length without the fear of his playing any serious shots against you.

'Boycs' always liked to have a good look at what the ball was doing. And while he was doing that it was not too difficult to get into a rhythm with two or three overs which, more often than not, turned out to be two or three maidens. It was not so much that one was putting pressure on him – after all he was happy to bide his time and stay there all day, which he often did – but Boycott himself was putting pressure on the batsmen at the other end.

Just as they felt that they had to take more chances against the quick bowlers in an attempt to get the scoreboard moving, so they felt that they had to be more adventurous against the spinners. Certainly Phil Edmonds and I found that this was the case when we played against Yorkshire. And while we were not complaining, it was hard not to sympathize with some of the younger batsmen in the side.

Having made what his supporters will doubtless condemn as the ritual criticism of their hero, I have to say that every other detail of Boycott's game was immaculate. He was the master technician and as such he was always the batsman whose wicket you treasured more than anybody else's. Any spin bowler who actually managed to deceive him, either through the air or off the pitch, could be very proud of himself indeed. And if a young spinner did claim GB's scalp early in his career it gave him something to savour for the rest of his life.

Dennis Amiss is in the same mould as Boycott, which is only

to be expected since they began playing round about the same time and grew up together in both county and Test cricket.

Like Boycott, Dennis lets the ball come on to him, knowing the danger involved in stretching to meet it when there are close fielders just in front of the bat. But he does not commit himself quite as much to the front foot as Boycott did. Amiss is more half-cock, playing with his bat very close to his pad. He also tends to play very low, which gives him the ability to drop the ball down near his feet, depending on how close in the fielders are.

There are times, too, when Amiss will look to dominate rather more than Boycott did. Against the off spinner, he uses his feet to get down the wicket and try to drive him through the midwicket area or to get back and attempt to force him through the offside. Similarly, he will seek to hit the left arm spinner through the covers with the turn.

Generally speaking, however, Amiss is like Boycott and all the batsmen of their generation in that he is content to wait for the loose ball. He does not try to make good balls into bad ones; he is prepared to let the bowler make the mistakes. That kind of attitude makes them very frustrating batsmen to bowl against.

Just as Amiss is that little bit different from Boycott, so their contemporary, Keith Fletcher, is slightly different again. In my opinion, he is the most effective player of spin bowling of the three for the basic reason that he is not content simply to occupy the crease but is looking to score runs all the time – even if it is only in singles.

Like Boycott and Amiss, he uses his feet to get on to the front foot but he plays very well off the back foot as well – and especially against the off spinners. At least that is the way he always looks to play me, just working the ball round the corner for a single most of the time but also sweeping (very well) if he is given the chance. For that specific reason, I try not to give him too much room.

Fletcher also has an interesting method against the left arm spinner. He seems to play forward defensively with a very closed face of the bat and if the wicket turns a bit and he is beaten a couple of times he will become more aggressive. Then, if there is the slightest degree of width, he will strike the ball on the up to try to get rid of the fielder at silly mid off.

Boycott, Amiss and Fletcher . . . three batsmen at the end of their careers but still, to my mind, the best three players of spin bowling in the country as they approached their retirement. It should have been part of any up-and-coming spinner's education to watch them play – and even better to bowl against them.

Bowling spin against batsmen of their quality, batsmen who were not looking to take the bowler apart but allowed him to bowl at them, gave the youngster a chance to develop his craft. He could learn how to bowl length and line without the threat of being smashed into the next county, probe for weaknesses in the knowledge that his opponent was relishing the contest as much as he was.

Sadly, it is not like that any more. My top three all developed their techniques in the early Sixties when the pace of the game was very different from what it is today.

The one-day game and bonus points in the first 100 overs of county matches have made batsmen much more aggressive. Nowadays they simply do not allow young spinners to bowl well at them – and certainly not in long spells. They go on the attack, dominating them, even bullying them, forcing them to vary their line and length, making them bowl badly. And that, I submit, is one of the main reasons why there are so few spinners coming through to command places in their county sides.

I like to think that I have the necessary experience to cope with the challenge – but I would probably have shrivelled if I had had to start my first-class career against the likes of Mike Gatting, Graham Gooch and Ian Botham, my pick as the three

most devastating players of spin bowling among modern
English batsmen.

Gatting's belligerent attitude towards all spin bowlers is
quite intimidating. He goes bustling in ready to sweep them, hit
them straight over the top or give himself room to cut them.
And when a spinner is confronted by someone like that, who
can hit him on both sides of the wicket, it makes bowling very
difficult indeed.

It is not so bad when a dominating batsman is hitting the ball
on only one side of the wicket – but it is a lot more awkward
when you have got a player such as 'Gatt' smashing it to all
points of the compass. And like Gooch and Botham, who have
pretty much the same attitude, he is also into those little
'reverse sweeps' they employ these days to muck the spinners
up and make them change their field placings. All in all, it can
be very frustrating.

The only thing the spinner can do in the circumstances is to
concentrate even harder on making sure it is the batsman who
makes the biggest error of judgement and not the bowler. He is
trying to force you to make the mistake of changing your length
and line. What you must do is keep bowling as straight as you
can and deny him any width at all. That way you are looking for
him to make the mistake because if he does miss the ball you
will have every chance of either bowling him or getting an lbw
decision.

It doesn't help, of course, if the batsman knows exactly what
you are trying to do; and that puts me at a considerable
disadvantage when I am bowling to Gooch, who probably
knows even more about me and my methods than Gatting
does.

When I go on tour with England, I don't enjoy bowling in
the nets because I am reluctant to give too much away to the
batsmen I have to play against in county cricket at home. In fact
I normally bowl seamers for that very reason. But Graham is a
very close friend of mine so when we went to South Africa

together in 1982 I used to spend a lot of time bowling my spinners to him in the nets.

It was a mistake that has cost me dearly. In our early days – playing 2nd XI and then county cricket for Middlesex and England respectively – I could bowl to him without too many problems and get him out fairly regularly. But it all changed after that trip to South Africa. By the time we came back, he knew all my secrets, and over the past four or five years I have not had much success against him. He has worked out a way of playing me based on upsetting my length and line (which he knows is my greatest strength) and it works very well for him.

Basically he plays me off the back foot, which the best players can do, especially in England where the wickets are so slow, and by doing that he forces me to pitch the ball up a bit more – so that he can then come forward and drive!

Sometimes he will feign to come down the pitch and then go back and play me off the back foot. Sometimes he will play a couple of risky shots through the offside and then, just when I think I am getting on top, he will hit me quite beautifully through mid on or midwicket. Sometimes he will force me to bring the fielders in by picking up a few singles – he does not just hit fours! – and then when they are there he will hit me over the top.

He does it all with such a casual air that I always feel that he is going to hit the ball up in the air at any moment. That has happened a few times in Test matches – but lately he has not done it against me very often.

If the mere presence of a Gatting or a Gooch is almost frightening to a spinner, then what about Botham, one of the most ferocious hitters ever to set foot on a cricket field?

In actual fact, Botham can get his head down and play spin bowling intelligently and well. He uses his pads a lot and will only bring the bat into play when he is deceived . . . or when he is seriously looking to hit the ball. When he does that, he hits it so hard that he can make the bowler and fielders cringe with the sheer power of it. He can hit it anywhere – long on, long off, deep midwicket, deep square leg, you name it – and a couple of sixes and two or three fours from him can change the complexion of any match.

I cannot remember 'Both' taking me apart too often – probably because I have not bowled against him that much! – but there was one memorable occasion when it took only one six to put me out of the attack and, I believe, decide the game.

It happened in the 1983 NatWest Trophy semi-final at Lord's when Botham played a true captain's innings to inspire a Somerset recovery from 52 for five to 222 for eight and victory over Middlesex by virtue of losing fewer wickets with the scores level.

The turning point, as far as I was concerned, came when I bowled an arm ball which did not drift away as I hoped but started going down the legside, and Botham simply picked it up and hit it for six. At the sight of that, Mike Gatting, in his first year as Middlesex captain, promptly took me off after just one over on the grounds that he could not risk the short boundary on the Tavern side – or the legside for the off spinner bowling with the slope from the pavilion end.

I did not bowl again until the last over by which time the scores were level and all 'Both' had to do was block it out for a maiden to win the match. He did it with great aplomb – even though he was on 96 at the time.

That was probably the most responsible innings Botham has ever played and certainly one of his most important for Somerset. There may have been more spectacular knocks when he has smashed quick hundreds and bombarded the surrounding streets with sixes. But that one took his side into a Lord's final, which they won by beating Kent, and did a tremendous amount not just for him but for Somerset cricket as well.

Yet, brilliantly as he played, I felt that a tactical error had cost us the game. Wilf Slack did take over from me to bowl nine overs for 26, but the fact was that we had wanted Botham to play shots against me, encouraging him to hit the ball in the air to give us a chance of getting him out.

I was sure that if we had persevered we would have got him out and gone on to win. And 'Gatt' admitted that he had got it wrong when he came up to me afterwards and said: 'Look, I think I made a mistake. You should have bowled.'

It was not the first time a captain must have bitterly regretted his fear of using a spin bowler against the mighty Botham. Australia's Kim Hughes doubtless felt the same way, only worse, at Headingley in 1981 when Botham hit that incredible 149 not out to change the course of the Ashes series. 'Both' blasted the Australian seamers to all parts yet Hughes completely ignored his only spinner, the left arm Ray Bright, until it was too late. When he did eventually bring Bright on, Botham found it a lot harder to strike the ball as cleanly as before. Suddenly he had to hit it rather than let it come on to the bat and he struggled more than at any stage of his innings. Unfortunately for Hughes and Australia, he had scored about 130 by then!

Having read what I think about the awesome task of confronting such merciless destroyers of spin bowling as Gatting, Gooch and Botham, you will be wondering by now who are the two young English batsmen whose very appearance through the pavilion gate fills me with dread.

I suppose I should not be admitting it because now they will probably make me suffer even more. But they are Paul Johnson, the nuggety little Nottinghamshire batsman, and Paul Smith, the big, blond all-rounder who plays for Warwickshire. I have no idea what other spin bowlers think about them but every time I see them coming to the wicket I say to myself: 'Oh, no . . . get somebody else on to bowl.'

I was not surprised to learn that young Johnson once smashed 195 not out – including sixteen sixes! – in a schools match. He only made his county debut in 1982 but he has already given me quite a bit of trouble for the infuriating reason that he will keep hitting the ball to places where he shouldn't. He uses his feet to get down to the pitch of it and lifts it over the top or drives it through the covers, he gets back and cuts it square on the offside, he sweeps backward of square. The ball just keeps flying all over the place.

You think to yourself: 'What on earth am I going to do about this bloke?' Your experience tells you that the ball should not be going where it is going, so you carry on bowling where you think you should be bowling. But still the ball keeps disappearing. It squirts off here, it squirts off there – yet all the time it seems to be squirting off the middle of the bat.

Paul Smith, who is still young enough to develop into a considerable all-rounder, is a little bit different from Johnson, as he doesn't hit me all over the place at all. The problem with him is that he plays everything in between square leg and midwicket – and how he manages to get the ball through there I just do not know.

Basically his method is very correct in that he waits for the ball and lets it come on to the bat. But, no matter where you bowl it, he just keeps playing it in front of square on the legside, off front foot or back. I have tried to open him up a bit by bowling a little wider of the off stump to get him driving with the bat away from the pad, but if the length is only slightly too full it becomes a half-volley, which he puts away without hesitation. Then, as soon as you start bowling a bit straighter again, he is back in the groove between square leg and midwicket.

It all seems a bit hard to take at the time. But I must say it is good to see two young English batsmen with so much natural ability, and it will be very interesting to observe how they progress in the next year or so. The amount of one-day cricket we play has changed attitudes in the game, especially among the younger batsmen who quickly discover that they cannot afford to get bogged down and must learn to work the ball around. More than that, however, I think the forthright

approach of young players like Johnson and Smith is an
example of how cricket reflects changing attitudes to life in
general.

I first noticed a difference in the kind of person coming into
the game when two very confident young men called Mike
Gatting and Ian Gould joined the Middlesex staff in 1975. Little
more than ten years later they were almost part of the
establishment as captains of Middlesex (and England) and
Sussex respectively. Yet they were – and, in many ways, still
are – typical of a new breed of cricketer.

It is most noticeable in the dressing room where the younger
players have a lot more to say for themselves nowadays. They
are cocky, chirpy and much less inhibited than they used to be.
There are none of the old cliques that senior players once
formed among themselves. Everything is out in the open. If
there is something to say, someone will say it. And that can only
be good for the game – even if such lack of inhibition is no good
at all for the spin bowler!

Test cricket presents an even greater challenge to the
spinner than county cricket does for three basic reasons. You
are up against much better players on much better wickets
under much more pressure. And you only had to watch the
likes of Allan Border and Viv Richards playing for Essex and
Somerset respectively to know how much better those players
are.

For one reason or another, I have played most of my Test
matches against Australia and the West Indies – and I seem to
have spent most of my time bowling against either Border or
Richards. So I suppose it is only natural that I should consider
them to be my most formidable opponents.

In fact, if I had to name the best overseas batsmen I have ever
bowled against it would be neither of those two, great as they
are, but Barry Richards, the incomparable South African opener
who played so magnificently for Hampshire between 1968 and
1978. Sadly, politics restricted him to only four Tests – all against

Australia in 1969–70 – so I never bowled to him at that level. But from what I have seen of him, he was not only the finest strokeplayer in the world but had a batting technique every bit as good as Boycott's. There can be no higher praise than that.

While Barry Richards was being condemned to pursuing his career as a cricketing mercenary, I was virtually growing up with Border in the international game. My first tour to Australia in 1978–9 was AB's first home series and although he soon found himself fighting a losing battle to save Australia from defeat – as he seems to have been doing most of the time since! – it was obvious from the outset that he was a very good player of spin. He played particularly well on the turning wickets at Sydney and I quickly realized that, in my own interests, I had better work out a method of bowling to him.

As with all good players of spin bowling, Border's 'secret' is his footwork. He is prepared to use his feet to get to the pitch of the ball and drive it to mid on, mid off or even over the top. And he is just as good off the back foot, punching the ball away on the offside or working it round to leg to mess up the spinner's length.

I have decided that the best way I can bowl to him is from over the wicket. If I go round the wicket, which many off spinners like to do against a left hander, he will be straight down the pitch looking to hit me through the offside. But if I bowl over the wicket, he is not quite as confident about giving me the charge because he is not so used to that line. And if I can pitch the ball around his leg stump or just outside, he can be in trouble if there is just a little bit of turn.

The only drawback to bowling over the wicket to the left hander is that there is not too much rough outside his leg stump for the off spinner to bowl into, because there are not that many left arm over-the-wicket bowlers around. So, with the wicket fairly flat, you only have to be slightly off line and he has got a free hit such as a sweep or a pull. That is why it is so important to get your line exactly right.

The main object of the exercise is to put pressure on him – because if AB has a fault it is that he cannot bear to think of himself or his team being dominated by spin bowling. When that happens, he will often have a rush of blood to the head, take a risk and play one or two rash shots. If it doesn't come off, then he has gone . . . as happened on two memorable occasions against Phillippe Edmonds, once when he charged down the wicket at Old Trafford and got himself stumped, and again when he tried to hit the left arm spinner out of the ground at Brisbane and was caught at cover point. But if Border does manage to get away with his moment of madness, then he flows.

It is probably because of that one mental weakness that Allan is at his best when Australia have their backs to the wall and he is forced to play with the utmost responsibility. At those times, he is brilliant. He will block, letting the ball come on to the bat instead of making the old Australian mistake of pushing at it; he will use his feet to hit the ball over the top to force the fielders back and take a bit of pressure off himself; he will get back to cut or sweep; and he will work the singles to keep the score ticking over.

When he is playing like that, he is as difficult as anybody to bowl to – as I discovered to my cost when he was scoring successive centuries against us at Perth and Adelaide. In that mood and with little in the wicket, you really do have to produce something special to get him out.

If Border becomes a bit belligerent when he thinks the spinners are beginning to get on top, then all I can say about Viv Richards is that he gets absolutely furious. He will not allow any spinner to bowl to him for more than a few overs before he is trying to smash him all round the ground. And he is even worse if the wicket shows any sign of spin and he gets a ball that actually turns a bit. Then he will really go on the rampage with a view to getting the spinner taken off – or, alternatively, making him wish he had been!

I had first hand experience of that kind of mayhem in the final Test in the West Indies in 1986. I felt that at long last we were beginning to get on top and might even have a chance of avoiding a 'whitewash' in the series when Viv sauntered on to his beloved Antigua Recreation Ground as though he owned the place and simply took the game by the scruff of the neck with the fastest century in Test history in terms of balls received.

He needed only 61 balls – but just one of those was enough to convince me of the impossibility of bowling against him that day. I thought that I had completely deceived him in flight (in fact, to this day, I am sure I had) when he was shaping to give himself a little room and hit me for yet another six over long off. I had bowled it a fraction shorter, a little bit straighter and more towards middle and leg. And, for an instant, I had him in two minds. Then, halfway through his original shot, he decided not to hit the ball over long off after all and just went round with the bat to pick it up and lift me nonchalantly over square leg for six.

It was then that I thought to myself: 'Well, bugger this! What am I doing bowling anyway? It's about time somebody else had a go.'

Ian Botham and I had taken the brunt of Viv's onslaught ('Both' went for 78 in 15 overs; I conceded 83 in 14) and afterwards it was suggested to our captain, David Gower, that the bowling might have been shared around a little bit more. It was a great knock to see – unless you happened to be watching it from where I was!

That was one of those occasions when the bowler's task was hopeless. But there have been other times when I believed that I had a reasonable chance of getting him out. Viv plays the off spinner to leg a lot of the time, especially early in his innings, and you do feel that you might pick him up if the ball holds up a little.

The trouble is that he does not give you very long to grab

your opportunity. He will soon be starting to give himself room to hit you square on the offside or loft you over mid off and extra cover. And before you know it, he has created havoc with your fielding placings and you have lost control over your line and length because you are trying to bowl more defensively.

All the captain can do in that situation is to take the spinner off and put a different bowler on – and then, perhaps, bring the spinner back half an hour later and make a fresh start. The fact is that once Viv has got on top of a particular bowler it is virtually impossible to bowl to him. The ball can go for six anywhere in the ground – and that is what makes him the most fearsome batsman in the world.

Yet there was a time when I would much rather have bowled to Viv Richards than Gordon Greenidge. Gordon and I had played together for South of England Schools in 1967 but he seemed to have no respect for me at all when I started my first-class career with Middlesex, and I used to hate being brought on to bowl against him.

Gordon, who went to school in Reading and could have played for England if he had not opted for his native West Indies, was the most difficult batsman I had ever bowled against. He dominated me, even bullied me, from the moment I came on. He is only a year older than I am but he already had all the shots – and he used them. He would hit the ball all round the wicket, sweeping, square cutting, late cutting, driving over long on and long off, pulling over midwicket. And a young spin bowler facing a barrage like that tends to lose all recognition of what is going on around him.

Fortunately for me, Middlesex had Mike Brearley as captain at the time and he kept a tight rein on things. He knew that once Gordon got cracking he had to take me off and let somebody else have a bowl at him. If he could get Gordon out of the way, then he could bring me back to start work on another batsman.

I don't know whether it is because Greenidge has mellowed

a bit or I have become a better bowler, but he has certainly been slightly more restrained against me in recent years. Not only that, he also seems to respect me a little more. And, as the seasons have gone by and I have become more aware of what is happening on the field and what the batsman is trying to do, I seem to have overcome my Greenidge phobia.

He will still try to boss me about early on just as he used to do. But if he finds he cannot get away with it he will settle for a more patient approach, playing sensibly and waiting for the bad ball. I must admit, however, that it is always at the back of my mind that if I don't keep on top of him he will murder me.

Having suffered so much at the hands of Richards and Greenidge, it is nice to know that I have already earned a measure of respect from Richie Richardson, who has always seemed destined to be the next in line of the great West Indian batsmen. Richie is a superb player of quick bowling in the Caribbean (though, as yet, he is not so good in England where the ball moves around a lot more) but he is nothing like as happy against spin. So when we were in the West Indies in 1986, it was quite amazing that not until I had got him out four or five times did we suddenly realize that he had usually amassed a big score before I even came on to bowl.

In fact I dismissed him six times on the trot in the Tests and, if you add a one-day international in between, seven times in eight knocks. He had made 102 in Trinidad and 160 in Barbados but he did not get quite as many after that and finished the series in a bit of a quandary. He had tried to attack me and he had tried to play me defensively, but each time I had claimed his wicket – and that kind of thing can have a deep mental effect on a batsman.

This can only be good for English cricket . . . and especially for English spinners. Richie already has a magnificent Test record and is obviously one of the players on whom the West Indies are basing their future. So it is a reassuring thought that an England off spinner can bowl to him without too much fear of being taken apart – and with high hopes of actually getting him out.

The Indians, of course, were brought up to play spin bowling – or at least they used to be – and you only have to look at a master batsman like Sunil Gavaskar to see how much a player can benefit from such an education. The way Gavaskar plays a spinner is just poetry in motion. He refuses to get flustered against any variety of spin in any situation . . . which is not all that surprising, really, when you remember that he learned his cricket playing with and against Bishen Bedi, Bhagwat Chandrasekhar, Erapally Prasanna and Venkataraghavan.

That kind of experience enabled Sunny to polish his skills to such a degree that he has no fear of any spin bowler – for the simple reason that he knows he has lived with the best. He just waits for the bad ball, supremely confident that he can dispatch it wherever he wants, be it over the top, square or through the onside with a whippy style which sends it racing past square leg with amazing power. Add to that his Boycott-like concentration and you can understand why a spinner does not have many chances to get him out.

It is an indication of how much the game has changed, even on the subcontinent, that the new generation of Indian batsmen do not play spin anything like as competently or as confidently as Gavaskar and his contemporaries used to do. The obvious reason is that India, in common with all the other Test-playing countries, is not producing quality spinners any more.

After the enduring Gavaskar, Dilip Vengsarkar and Mohammad Azharuddin are probably their best batsmen at the moment and I have a lot of respect for both of them. I did not go to India in 1984–5 when Azharuddin became the first batsman ever to score centuries in each of his first three Tests, but he is obviously a fine, wristy player who seems to play spin reasonably well. Vengsarkar can be an excellent player of slow bowling on wickets that do not turn too much, as he showed with successive centuries at Lord's and Headingley in 1986. He looks to play everything through midwicket and when you bring the fielders up to close the gaps he will have a go over the top. He has great powers of concentration and refuses to give his wicket away – which is what Test cricket is all about.

Yet, despite their backgrounds and the fact that most of them have seen quite a lot of spin bowling from a very early age, Vengsarkar, Azharuddin and the rest of the Indian batsmen seem to struggle as badly as anybody when they are confronted by a turning wicket.

I well remember the Edgbaston Test in 1986 when Phillippe Edmonds got four wickets for next to nothing in the second innings. Some of the Indians didn't seem to have a clue against him. Ravi Shastri, another player with a fine Test record as a batsman, was so desperate that he went charging down the wicket, got a thick edge and was caught in the gully. And Vengsarkar, fresh from his first innings century, pushed at a turning delivery and was well caught behind by wicketkeeper Bruce French. They were both out trying to play shots they should never have been playing against the spinning ball.

I find it surprising that spin bowlers can dominate Indian batsmen – and Pakistanis, come to that. But Javed Miandad is a rather different kettle of fish. I have not played a lot of cricket against Javed at either Test or county level so it is difficult to assess him technically but, from what I have seen on the odd occasion I have bowled to him, I am sure he is a very high class player of spin.

He is the kind of player who is determined to dominate you. And he tends to do it with some style. He will play, play, play . . . then, all of a sudden, he will come charging down the wicket and put you through midwicket or extra cover or over the top.

As ever, the key to it all is footwork. Javed is very quick and very difficult to anticipate from the bowler's point of view because he comes so late. Most experienced spinners can sense from any slight movement of the batsman before the ball is delivered that he is coming down the wicket and have time to adjust their length accordingly. But with Javed there are no early warning signs. You can come up and bowl an ordinary, good length ball and, in a flash, he is down there at the pitch of it.

It sounds a bit daft, I know, but I do believe that good batsmen play good bowlers better than they play bad bowlers – because they know where the ball is going to pitch. Against a good off spinner in full control of his line and length, the good batsman can actually go down the wicket confidently because he knows that the ball will pitch in a certain area. Against a lesser spinner whose line and length vary, it is much more difficult to go down the pitch with the same degree of confidence. This can make life a bit difficult for a bowler like myself who relies on his ability to apply pressure through sheer accuracy. All I can do against the Javed Miandads of this world is to trust my instincts to give me a clue as to his intentions.

It is strange how all the great players around the world have their own particular ways of playing spin bowling – and it is frightening to contemplate what kind of 'Super Batsman' would be produced if you could combine all their special qualities. Just imagine it . . . Viv Richards's power and aggression, Sunil Gavaskar's skill and artistry, Allan Border's determination and tenacity, Javed Miandad's flair and footwork, Geoff Boycott's technique and concentration.

It would be fantastic to watch him play – as long as I was not the bowler!

How's That, Umpire?

BY NOW YOU will be well aware that I am blatantly biased in favour of spinners – but I think it fair to say that they need a bit more luck than other types of bowlers to be successful. In many cases, they have to be extremely fortunate just to get a bowl at all. And, as I am forever telling anybody who cares to listen, you cannot be expected to take wickets when you are not bowling.

Where we are lucky in England, however, is in the general standard of our umpiring, which is so vitally important if the spinner is to get his just rewards. Without a doubt, our umpiring is the best in the world for the simple reason that the vast majority of the umpires have played first-class cricket themselves. With very few exceptions, they know the players and the players know them, and that leads to a good rapport which can only be for the good of the game.

In this instance, familiarity does not breed contempt so much as mutual respect, and this may be seen and heard any day of the week in all the good-natured banter which goes on in county cricket. Talking to umpires is very much frowned upon overseas, and you have to be very careful if you say anything at all. In England, you can have a laugh and a joke with them by suggesting that there is a big difference between what you have seen and what they have seen . . . even though you both know that you have seen exactly the same thing.

'Oh!' you might exclaim in mock surprise after having an lbw appeal turned down. 'Was that missing off stump?'

'No,' the umpire will reply. 'Missing leg!'

Or, when the ball is really turning and the batsman is

repeatedly being struck on the pad, you might inquire: 'How many straight balls have I got to bowl before you are going to give him out?'

You have to be fairly selective, of course, because one or two of the umpires might take such remarks the wrong way. Alan Whitehead, for example, can be a bit strait-laced in that respect but with men such as David Constant, Dicky Bird and Barrie Meyer there is always time for a bit of fun as long as the situation is not too tense.

This may all sound somewhat trivial in the context of what is now a highly professional sport, but there is a serious aspect to it as well. It shows that players and umpires are on the same wavelength, which means that they interpret the Laws of Cricket in the same way, whereas in other parts of the world there is not the same level of understanding and they can interpret them entirely differently.

I imagine that kind of thing happens in most sports, and especially ball sports, but certainly in cricket umpiring inter-pretations do vary alarmingly. In Australia, New Zealand, the West Indies, India, Pakistan, Sri Lanka and South Africa there is a world of difference between the standard of their umpiring and ours – and spin bowlers are particularly affected because there is so little margin for error.

It can be very disconcerting in Australia, for instance, where a batsman can be half forward on the flattest of wickets, which is never going to turn or even bounce very much, and get struck on the pads without being in the slightest danger of being given out lbw. Yet if an off spinner is bowling wicket to wicket, getting very close to the stumps, as I do, and making the ball pitch in line and then skid on, he must have a very good chance of getting most batsmen out lbw even if they are playing forward.

It is even more galling when you see a batsman come half forward, no more than a foot in front of the crease, and more or less kick the ball away with the bat behind the pad, making no attempt to play a stroke. They would not get away with that in England because the umpire just wouldn't stand for it.

They call it 'giving the batsman the benefit of the doubt', which is a term you hear wherever cricket is played. Yet the best umpire will tell you that there is no such thing as the benefit of the doubt. There is no doubt in their minds. The batsman is either out or he is not out.

I am sure that it is all down to experience – and to the fact that they do not play anything like as much cricket anywhere overseas as we do in England. Overseas umpires therefore have far more sympathy with batsmen who do not get the opportunity to play too many innings during a season. Certainly in grade cricket in Australia, batsmen sometimes don't know when their next knock is going to come. It could be in two, three or, if there is bad weather in between, even four weeks' time – which helps to explain why so many of them are disinclined to 'walk' when they know full well that they are out.

This puts an extra onus on the umpires, the vast majority of whom have never played first-class cricket. Indeed some of them have never played cricket at any level at all. They just love the game and, perhaps because of their lack of ability as players, have taken up umpiring to be part of it.

I am not saying that all overseas umpires are hopeless. In fact some of them are very knowledgeable and efficient. But I do wonder if they can possibly have the same kind of understanding of what a bowler, and specifically a spin bowler, is trying to do as someone like John Hampshire, the former England, Yorkshire and Derbyshire batsman who joined the umpires' list after playing in nearly 600 first-class matches.

Far from being intimidated by the prospect of being put under pressure, he actually relished the opportunity of standing in quite a few Middlesex matches early in his umpiring career because he knew that we had a good bowling side, including two spinners, and that there would be a lot of men around the bat and plenty of tight situations. He thought it was a better test of his umpiring ability than being involved with less competitive bowling sides who did not generate so many incidents involving appeals.

One wonders how many relatively inexperienced overseas umpires would have felt the same way. Would they really have understood what the off spin bowler was trying to do? Would they have known that when he was bowling close to the stumps he was trying to make the ball pitch in line and go straight on rather than pitch outside the off stump and turn? Would they have noticed if he had gone wide of the crease or slipped in the arm ball?

Certainly not in South Africa. It was impossible for me to get an lbw decision there for the simple reason that the umpires were down on their haunches with their noses just above the stumps. They were so low down that by the time they had looked up from watching your front foot to make sure you were not over-stepping the crease, all they could see was the batsman's pad. They did not have a clue what kind of delivery you had just bowled or what the ball was doing up in the air. Just because I was an off spinner, they imagined that every ball I bowled was going to turn – so if it pitched in line with the stumps they automatically assumed that it was going to go down the legside.

They are not quite as bad as that in the Test-playing countries, but the general standard of umpiring around the world must definitely be improved. That is why I am in favour of an international panel of umpires.

The players who would suffer most from that – initially, at any rate – would be the England players because we would have fewer English umpires standing in our matches and interpreting the laws in the same way that we do. But I totally agree with the principle and welcomed the experiment with neutral umpires in the last World Cup in India and Pakistan.

I thought that the scheme they had a few years ago, whereby

umpires from other countries were co-opted on to the first-class list in England and stood in county matches, was an excellent idea and should be considered again. It could only be to the advantage of a couple of Australia's better umpires like Steve Randell and Tony Crafter – or even the 18-year-old from Tasmania who was already umpiring first-class matches when we were there – to gain more experience by coming to England and working alongside our leading officials.

English umpires can teach their overseas counterparts a tremendous amount. I know that Dicky Bird has travelled extensively to talk to umpires and address their associations; and I have seen for myself what a magnificent job Barrie Meyer has been doing on his visits to South Africa over the past three or four years.

He had not been there long when he went to umpire a club match at the famous Wanderers ground at Johannesburg. A batsman got a big outside edge and was caught at first slip. Everyone appealed but the batsman just stood his ground and showed not the slightest inclination to leave the crease.

Barrie didn't do or say anything . . . until the bowler, understandably disgruntled, had slowly returned to his mark and was preparing to come in again. Then umpire Meyer just put out an arm to stop him and, in a voice loud enough for everyone on the field to hear, said to the batsman:

'Are you going to walk? Or am I going to have to give you out?'

At that, the fielders collapsed into fits of laughter . . . and the batsman was so embarrassed that he had to go. It was a perfect example of the kind of action that is needed to give batsmen the message in no uncertain terms.

There was embarrassment of a different kind in the fourth Test between Australia and England at Melbourne in 1986. I was bowling when the ball went up in the air off opening batsman Geoff Marsh's glove and Bill Athey caught it at short leg. Geoff – or 'Swampy' as the cricketers call him – wanted to go but, like any true blue Aussie, he waited for the umpire's decision. And when the umpire gave him not out, he stayed.

'Look,' Marsh told me afterwards, 'it was such a delicate situation that I couldn't go. I was too embarrassed.'

That sort of episode does nobody any good. We all had a go at 'Swampy', who happens to be a genuinely nice guy, and he got himself into such a state that he ran himself out off the very next ball. Then we gave him a lot more stick as he was going off. When you get that kind of aggression against that kind of player, the umpire must realize that he has made a mistake.

You do get some decisions that go the other way, of course, like those little bat–pad 'catches' you are given when you have already started to appeal and suddenly think to yourself that the batsman has not touched it after all. Then there are the odd occasions when the fielders around the bat know that the batsman has nicked the ball but no one else is aware of it.

That happened at Melbourne, too. Peter Sleep went for a drive and, apparently, got a faint nick which took the pad and again went to Athey at short leg. All the close fielders went up in a confident appeal but I had not heard the nick so I couldn't expect the umpire to have heard it, either.

Incidents like that one, however, are pretty rare. Generally speaking, I do believe that the standard of umpiring must be improved world-wide. Apart from anything else, it can have a crucial bearing on a bowler's career. In a match, there is a big gap between three for 40 and six for 40. When you look back at the end of a tour and think of this chance that went down and that chance that went down and two or three 'plumb' lbw decisions which were not given, you are talking about half a dozen or more wickets you didn't get. And that can make all the difference between a rather ordinary tour and a highly successful one.

So I am all for an international panel of umpires – even in England, despite the predictable hue and cry from some of our

Two more old masters. Dennis Amiss
and Geoff Boycott always played a game
of patience against the spinner but
when the bad ball arrived they put it
away, Amiss (left) square on the offside,
Boycott (below) with a sweep – one of
his favourite shots.

Skippers under stress. David Gower (above) and Keith Fletcher (below) seem to have their problems as they ponder what to do next; but I found them both more sympathetic to the spinner than either Ian Botham or Bob Willis, seen here trying to understand precisely what Vic Marks wants (right).

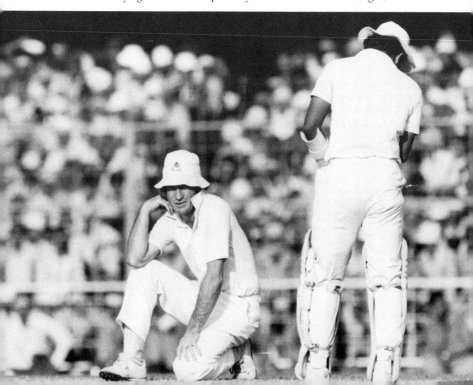

My most formidable opponents in international cricket. I seem to have spent most of my Test career bowling against Viv Richards (left) 'the master blaster'...

...and Allan Border (right), who has battled so hard to try to inspire his Australian side.

leading officials about the effect it would have on their international careers.

We may have the best umpires in the world but they still make a lot of mistakes; and in my experience as an England player over the past two or three years, too many of those mistakes have gone against us. In fact, I would go so far as to suggest that when it has come to a marginal decision, the opposition has got the verdict six times out of ten. The umpires would never agree, of course, but what I am saying is that there is suspicion on both sides and the time has surely come for something to be done about it.

The answer may be to follow the example of tennis, which now has a team of full-time professional umpires travelling the world for all the major championships. They have been appointed in conjunction with the players, who are naturally more prepared to accept their decisions. The same kind of thing could happen in cricket.

The Old Master

NO ONE KNOWS better than my old mentor Fred Titmus how much the game has changed for the spin bowler. When he played his first game for Middlesex at the age of 16 in 1949, county cricket was played on uncovered wickets and there was no such thing as the one-day game. When he played his last game at the age of 49 in 1982, pitches were covered and three one-day competitions played over 40, 55 and 60 overs made totally different demands on the players and especially the spinners.

Fred, one of the few players to play first-class cricket over a period of five decades, was equal to all the changes. He did the double of 1,000 runs and 100 wickets in a season eight times, took more than 100 wickets in a further 15 seasons, took 10 or more in a match 20 times and over five in an innings 168 times. And all that despite losing three toes in a boating accident in the West Indies in 1968.

How I envy him those figures – and how I envy all those spinners who were bowling 25 years ago. As an example just look at the averages at the end of the 1954 season. Of the top 50 bowlers in the County Championship, no fewer than 20 of them were spinners. Bruce Dooland, the great Australian leg spinner who played for Nottinghamshire, was the top wicket-taker with 196 while Johnny Wardle had 155, Bob Appleyard 154, Jim Laker 135 and Tony Lock 134. Five more spinners took more than 100 wickets, including Fred Titmus himself whose 111 at 20 apiece were only good enough to give him 38th place in the averages.

It was a rather different situation when Fred became a
selector in the Eighties; so when we went to Trent Bridge for a
Test match against the West Indies at a time when there was
not a single spinner in the top 20 in the averages, I sought him
out for a chat about the basics of his bowling to try to find out
how much his views differed from mine. We had quite a lot in
common, including the fact that we had both bowled seamers
in our early days, and I began by asking him:

John Emburey: Let's talk about your early career which was a
real mixture of spin bowling and seam bowling. How much did
the seam bowling help you?
Fred Titmus: Quite a lot, I think. I can remember being sent to
Alf Gover's cricket school at Wandsworth in the winter of
1949 when I was 17 to develop seam bowling rather than off
spin. I think there had been a mistake somewhere along the
line! But it did me a lot of good. Alf taught me that the one
great asset for any bowler whether you were quick or slow was
to reach as high as you could when you actually got to the
crease and bowl from as high as you could. That gave you a
good, upright action which a slow bowler has got to have. I
think it's very important and if a slow bowler is ever having a
bit of a problem I always recommend going into the nets and
bowling some seam. You get a better swing of the arm and
things like that. That is, I think, the most important bit of
advice ever given to me and I'll always be grateful to Alf for it.
JE: It plays a big part in the pivoting and the follow-through,
doesn't it?
FT: Of course it does. And another thing bowling seamers does
is to give you a bigger range. You can go from bowling a quick
ball to bowling a slow one, whereas if you've never bowled
seamers your quick ball is not that quick. Certainly in my early
days I used to bowl a lot of middle and leg yorkers from wide
of the crease and get a lot of wickets with them. By bowling
seam, you also develop the away swinger. If you're bowling off

breaks they call it drift, but if you've bowled seam you know how to do it. Otherwise you've just got to learn as you go along.

JE: You're about 5 ft 9 in in height. What would your advantages or disadvantages be compared with me at 6 ft 2 in in bowling terms, i.e. length, trajectory and, perhaps, pace? Or would that be determined by the type of wicket you were playing on?

FT: People talk about this a lot but I don't think it makes an awful lot of difference how tall you are. The only thing from the point of view of a person of my height – five or six inches shorter than you – is that the ball always had to be going up when it left my hand whereas somebody like yourself can get a little bit of loop without the ball going up. Sometimes, strangely enough, the fact that the shorter chap does have to toss the ball up helps it bounce a little bit more on a hard wicket than a taller bloke who has to bowl it in. But I don't think it matters all that much. There have been a lot of great Indian spinners, Pakistani spinners, even English spinners who have been short but I cannot see that it makes a significant difference.

JE: Do you think the fact that you had to make the ball go up in the air a bit more made it easier for you to vary your length?

FT: Oh, yes, I think that must be so. Once the ball goes up in the air it means that the batsman has to wait a fraction longer for it to come down. In that respect, I think it must be harder for someone tall to bowl slow although I don't really know. It's just an assumption on my part. And people do change. Ray Illingworth, who must be getting on for six feet, got slower – and possibly better – as he got older. I think that when we were young we all bowled the ball fairly quickly for off spinners. People think that we were always slow bowlers who gave the ball a lot of air but I can assure you that until we were about 35 we did push the ball along at a reasonable pace.

JE: So it was only in the later stages of your career that you

actually slowed down in pace and relied on your guile and
experience to get people out?

FT: That's right. As you get older, you're not quite as quick . . .
mainly because you don't have as much energy!

JE: Now you played for most of your career on uncovered
wickets. Do you think they were good for the development of
the spinner or do you think the covered wickets we have today
are more advantageous?

FT: I think uncovered wickets are good for the spinner because
they teach you more about how to bowl. These days spin
bowlers feel they are under pressure once the ball starts to turn
and people suddenly expect them to get the wickets. A lot of
them don't like bowling on turning wickets because their
length has to be more exact and they're not quite sure of their
accuracy.

JE: That's true. I was someone who didn't enjoy bowling on
wet wickets simply because I am a little bit taller than most
spinners and my length is a fraction shorter than theirs so that
on a wet wicket where the ball tends to stop and sit up a bit the
batsmen can get on the back foot and look to pull or sweep.

FT: Well, that's right, but the more you play, the more you
learn – and if you don't play on wet wickets you don't learn
how to bowl on them. But the one thing an off spinner or any
slow bowler, come to that, has got to have is control over his
length and direction. So if you play on a slow wicket you can
pitch it up and if it's a bit quicker you can pitch it shorter. I
found playing on uncovered wickets that there were days when
you had to bowl a yard shorter than on other days. But if you
played enough on these different types of wicket you were able
to adjust. It was only once in a blue moon that you found it very
difficult to do that.

JE: And obviously there is a lot more variation when wickets
are left uncovered – you get good ones, slow ones, wet
ones. . . .

FT: Exactly. And I've always thought the best thing a slow

bowler can have to cope with different conditions is accuracy. The degree of spin is not that important – as long as you turn the ball a certain amount, it hasn't got to be very much – but you must be in control of your length and be capable of pitching the ball where you want to pitch it.

JE: How much do you think that field placings have changed? Did your placement of the fielders vary very much or did you know what you were going to have and more or less stick to that?

FT: It varied with the pace of the wicket. I think I was one of the first – probably with Ray Illingworth – of the new breed of off spinners who did bowl a swinger or arm ball, as they call it now, and also spun the ball. They used to have four men in the covers in the old days because they bowled it somewhere like six inches outside the off stump, and a lot of the batsmen were great offside players. But when we came in about five years after the war, there was a big gap between us and the old off spinners. We started bowling the ball at the off stump or just outside it, and batsmen tended to look to play more on the onside, so we took the extra fielder away from the off and put him in at midwicket. It depended on how quick or how slow the wicket was exactly where we put him. In general, wickets were a little bit quicker than they are now and they used to bounce a bit more, so we always kept a slip in.

JE: When you say they bounced a bit more, was it because there was more grass on them or were they just harder and drier?

FT: They were harder. On most first-class grounds these days, you have to run up a little hill to bowl. That is because of the subsoil or top dressing which is not as hard as the other stuff. And there was no question that when wickets got wet I would hit batsmen on the glove as they played forward defensively. You don't see that now. And you don't see fields like we had with three short legs, two of them backward of square, because the ball used to fly. That just doesn't happen any more.

JE: And when you were bowling on slow wickets, when there was obviously not much pace or bounce, what sort of field placing did you have then? Would you be looking to be aggressive or just go on the defensive and wait for the batsman to come at you?

FT: Well, I normally reckoned that if you got a slow pitch, the ball was going to turn a bit, so obviously you were going to pitch the ball up a little more and probably bowl it slightly quicker. Sometimes it was a negative tactic. The more you pitched it up, the more batsmen were going to drive at you and you would probably get wickets. But once you see the ball turn, you tend to think of short legs, so you put people in close. And when you put people in close on a slow wicket, you do tend to pitch it up a bit more and bowl it a little quicker. Sometimes it is probably better – and this is a thing a bowler has got to recognize for himself – to be a little more defensive in your field and give the ball more air. The delicate decision is when to switch over.

JE: Do you think, then, that the modern day spinner tends to attack too much?

FT: Yes. No question about that. The one thing I don't like to see early on – and certainly not for a few overs – is a fielder in the silly mid off position because I think the bowler's natural reaction is to protect him a little bit. When you want to be pitching the ball up and giving it a bit of air, there's a chap there you naturally try to protect, so your line changes and you bowl straighter, which is not what you really want to be doing. Unless or until you're really in your stride, you're right on top, new batsmen are coming in and you've got a few runs to play with, I don't see that bloke as an advantage. In fact I see him as a disadvantage.

JE: That was just what I discovered when I first joined Middlesex. I'd never bowled with a silly mid off in school, club or even 2nd XI cricket and once I played a couple of games for the county side and the captain [Mike Brearley] introduced a silly mid off, I found that my whole line, length and even the pace I bowled changed. It was totally alien to me to bowl like that – and all because I wanted to protect the silly mid off.

FT: I know the captain you're talking about and I always used to disagree with him on this. Fortunately I was in a more senior position than you were and was old enough to get my own way. But that is an example of the captain needing to understand what the bowler is trying to do.

JE: I still disagree with 'Gatt' [Mike Gatting] on some of my field placings. But to some extent I'm in a similar position with him as you were with 'Brears'.

FT: I think it's essential that when a captain is dealing with a bowler who knows his stuff, he has to keep the bowler happy because it's the only way that he can bowl. You can't get him to bowl properly if he hasn't got the field he wants. He'll have a niggle about it in the back of his mind. And while Brearley was a very attacking captain I don't think that his tactics were always to the advantage of slow bowlers like Phillippe Edmonds and sometimes yourself. Certainly in the case of Edmonds, it did set him back.

JE: How much pressure a spinner can put on a batsman depends a lot on the captain. Most of the pressure goes on when the ball is turning and you're bowling well. But I can remember that when I was playing with you and someone like John Hampshire came in you knew he was going to hit you over midwicket and you wanted a man back there straightaway to stop him doing it – even though 'Brears' would still want that man up close. So you were actually trying to make the batsman play somewhere else. To what extent can you put pressure on like that?

FT: As you say, it depends on who is batting against you. There are some batsmen who will come in and see the ball turning and the short legs around the bat and say to themselves: 'Right, I've got to get rid of those or I'm going to get out', and immediately have a go at you. If they're going to do that, you've got to have a

man deep. It may look a bit silly but I always used to think that
it was better to have three men up and two out and no one in
the middle because it made the batsman think about what he
was going to do. Nowadays you see bowlers coming under
attack with men still around the bat and nobody out deep, and I
think that's a big mistake – against certain players anyway.

JE: One final question, Fred. What effect has the one-day game
had on the spin bowler?

FT: More effect than it should have done. People tend to look
at old bowlers like me and say: 'It was all right for you . . . you
never had to play one-day cricket.' In fact I did play one-day
cricket. I played something like ten years of it! And I gave it a
great deal of thought. I went through the whole range of things
like length and direction and the speed at which I bowled and
came to the conclusion that if I bowled fairly normally I would
be just as successful. What I think does make a difference in
one-day cricket is not so much how you bowl but when you
bowl. When we first started playing it, I used to come on at the
end because I was considered to be the steady bowler who
could slow the scoring rate down. That brought one of two
results. You either got four for 25 or nought for 60!

JE: Yes, that's similar to the way I bowl in one-day cricket
now – coming on at the end and not actually spinning the ball
but trying to bowl yorkers.

FT: That's right. But then after a while we had a rethink and I
would come on first change with the idea of slowing them
down early on so that they had to have a slog at the end. Either
way, I'm not convinced that the slow bowlers can't bowl in
one-day cricket. But having tried to bowl well up, having tried
to bowl leg stump and having tried to bowl off stump, I came to
the conclusion that the best way I could bowl was the way I
knew how to bowl.

And with that Fred confirmed my own feelings that the basics
of the game of cricket have not really changed all that much. It

is just that the demands of the limited-overs version have made it so much more difficult for the spin bowler. I don't believe that we theorize about it any more than they did, but the need to adjust to the various forms of cricket we play makes it far more awkward to develop and maintain a proper rhythm.

I certainly agree with what he says about the necessity for captains to understand what the spinners are trying to do – and particularly when it comes to the one-day game. Spinners can be successful but it all depends on when they bowl and how they are used. Middlesex's dramatic, two-run victory over Kent in the 1986 Benson and Hedges Cup Final provided a classic example of that. When Phillippe Edmonds came on first, he got hit, so I took over to try to keep it tight and managed to bowl 11 overs for only 17 runs. Then Phillippe came back when they were desperate for runs and picked up three important wickets. Thus two spinners were used in two different ways and both proved highly successful.

As for the wickets we play on these days, they are just not helping anybody. I have discussed this with Fred many times and he has confirmed that in his day they were generally much harder and drier. In too many cases nowadays I feel that their preparation is so bad and they have deteriorated so much that spinners are simply not being employed as they should be. The fast bowlers and medium-pacers are becoming more and more dominant – and the spinners are being pushed further and further into the background. And that is terribly sad.

Unlucky for Some

WHILE I COULD consider myself fortunate to have held my place in the England team for so long, two of my fellow off spinners were not so lucky.

Greg Matthews, 'the punk in the baggy green cap' as some people called him, who had become something of a cult figure in Australia, was dropped from the final Test against England in 1987 on his home ground at Sydney. To his enormous credit, he came back to bowl splendidly in the one-day internationals but was left out of Australia's World Cup-winning squad and obviously had a fight on his hands to regain his Test place from fellow New South Welshman Peter Taylor, who had taken over in quite sensational fashion.

Roger Harper, who I consider to be one of the most outstanding cricketing talents in the world today, is still battling to establish himself in the pace-dominated West Indies side and only got into the team in England in 1988 because of injuries to a couple of their batsmen.

I felt desperately sorry for both of them – not least because there are so few spin bowlers with their kind of ability coming through at the moment that selectors ought to be giving them every encouragement and not discouraging them in this way. It is hard enough for young spinners to establish themselves in England, but it must be even more difficult in countries which have based all their successes in recent years on fast bowling. I want to see spin bowling flourish everywhere in the cricketing world; so I approached both Matthews and Harper to chat about their problems, how they saw their roles in the modern game and what, in fact, they were trying to do from a bowling angle.

The day I caught up with Greg at his beloved Sydney Cricket Ground, he was tackling the duties of 12th man with all the enthusiasm he shows for his batting, bowling and fielding. Out in the middle, the previously unknown Peter Taylor was making a fairy-tale debut as Australia headed towards their first win in 15 Test matches. Yet every time Matthews emerged from the dressing room – whether he was going out to field as substitute, delivering a fresh pair of batting gloves or just carrying the drinks – he got a bigger cheer than any of the other players did.

It was good to hear. Cricket today needs personalities like Greg Matthews. Seeing someone with his character, his individuality and his extrovert sense of humour will encourage a lot of young Australians to emulate him. And that means, I hope, that they will want to be spin bowlers prepared to work at their craft rather than fast bowlers just wanting to run up and knock somebody's head off.

Matthews is very serious about his cricket – but he has also brought a lot of fun to the game; and that is the greatest thing about him. He so obviously enjoys his cricket and enjoying your sport must be what matters more than anything else.

Some people may find it easy to detract from what he has done in an Australian team of average ability, but his achievements should not be under-estimated. To make it to the top in any Test side is a considerable feat. He had already proved that he could perform, that he could compete, at the highest level. Now, having gone through a lean spell, he not only had to fight back himself, other people had to get behind him, encourage him, let him know that he was still a good player and give him back some of his confidence.

He had enjoyed a good home season against New Zealand and India the previous year and he had obviously done well, too, on tour to India. But it was always going to be difficult for him against an England team containing so many high quality batsmen who play spin quite well on wickets which are not turning very much. Sure enough, he struggled throughout the first four Tests, taking just two wickets at 147.5 runs apiece, and, sadly for him, his captain lost confidence in him. It was not merely that Matthews was not taking wickets; he was not doing a job for the side, either, by containing the batsmen and putting pressure on them so that they had to take more chances.

In his defence, I have to say that the Australians never attacked as much as England did and there were occasions when I disagreed with the way Allan Border handled his spinners – especially after Peter Sleep was added to the side, which should have made life easier for Matthews. There were certain times, for instance, when Border brought the spinners on straightaway against Chris Broad, which was clearly the right tactic, but I felt that he should have had a couple of men up close to the bat from the start as well.

Chris is becoming a better player of spin and looks quite secure once he is in, but he is still not the most confident batsman against spin early in an innings. Yet Border tended to put the close fielders in after he had offered the bat–pad chance rather than before – as it were, after the horse had bolted. It was similar to making the elementary mistake of following the ball around in the outfield and putting a fielder where the batsman has just hit it instead of getting hold of the bowler and telling him to bowl to his field.

It was because of the way that the Australian spinners had been handled that I felt so sad for Matthews when he was dropped for that final Test on the one pitch which we all knew was going to turn. As I have said, he loves Sydney and he is the type of bowler who bowls well there. Playing there would also have given his confidence a much-needed boost and I thought that the selectors should have considered that.

All things considered, it seemed unfortunate and a little unjust that a wholehearted cricketer, who had been rated quite highly as an off spinner, should be abruptly dropped for having had a lean spell, which can happen to anybody. The runs he had made in the meantime did not seem to help his cause because he was suddenly being talked about more as a batsman than a bowler.

It was hardly the right way to treat someone who may be very excitable but is also an excellent all-round cricketer who is always good to watch and, for all his antics, sets a marvellous example in the field. Apart from his chasing, catching and throwing, he never stops encouraging the bowlers. If one of them bowls a bad ball, he will scamper across and say: 'Aw, c'mon, don't worry about it, you can bowl, you can get through 'em.'

A lot of players lack confidence and belief in themselves when things are going wrong. Matthews tries to give them that. Unfortunately, there was no one to give Matthews confidence when things were going wrong for him – not even, apparently, his captain. So I began our conversation by asking Greg:

John Emburey: How important is the captain's role? How much does it influence the spinner – not just you, but spinners generally? For example, I think Allan Border has handled Peter Taylor well in this final Test, taking him off when batsmen have been looking to get after him, bringing him back when there has been a little bit more pressure on them and being rewarded with important wickets. What are your views?

Greg Matthews: The captain's role is very important for everyone – and for spinners it's crucial. Quick bowlers can basically run in and have that fear factor and try to knock people's heads off, whereas a spinner has to be more subtle, using – how do I say? – guile and trickery. You've just used the example of Peter . . . how when batsmen are getting after you and you've been taken for a few fours a captain will come up to you and slow the game down a bit, talk to you, tell you what he wants, give you a bit of confidence, discuss field placings.

Communication is vital. If you've just got a leader who throws you the ball and moves the field without communicating with you, it can be very disheartening. All of a sudden you can turn round and find that one of your bat–padders has gone. It's also very important that his knowledge of how to use spin bowling is quite high, because a captain who doesn't know how to use spin bowling can cost you a lot of wickets and lot of opportunities as well.

JE: And, because of that, you can very easily lose your place in the side . . .

GM: Yeah. Sure. Of course.

JE: Right. Now, when you're asked to bowl, whether it's in a one-day game, a four-day Sheffield Shield match or a Test, what are your first thoughts about what you're trying to do?

GM: I'm just trying to settle in, that's the most important thing when I come on to bowl. I usually try to get away with a maiden or something like that and just get my rhythm.

JE: Yes, I tend to do the same . . . try to bowl two or three maidens and work out the pace of the wicket, how much turn it's got and what I'm actually going to be trying to do. Then I can sort out the line and length I want to bowl and take it from there. Now, when you've been on for a while, at what stage do you start trying to vary your trajectory, your line and perhaps the degree of spin on the ball?

GM: It depends on the state of the game. I know that sounds a little vague but it does depend on what's happening at the time. If you're in need of quick wickets then obviously you're looking to do it pretty much straightaway – although Murray Bennett, the left arm spinner who plays with me for New South Wales, is a guy who is more consistent. He likes to get 'em in there, in the same mould as you, dare I say, even though you are a different type of bowler.

JE: You mean he likes to be at the batsman straightaway?

GM: Yeah. He plays more percentages. The main criticism of my bowling has always been that I try to take a wicket every ball, which is something I've tried to get out of this year. But it's all hearsay, I'm sure it depends on the state of the game. Here at Sydney, for example, one does tend to be more consistent – more boring, dare I say – because the wicket tends to help you a lot more. It's different on other grounds like the Adelaide Oval. Although I bowled poorly in the Test there, I don't mind bowling at Adelaide because you can get a bit of turn and bounce. And if you're on form and confident, it's a good wicket to bowl on because you can get a little funky with the things you're trying to do.

JE: So on wickets that turn a lot, you want less variation . . . you just want to be pitching it up more and looking to get the batsman coming forward and driving you?

GM: That's the important thing on spinning wickets – keeping the ball up there. You don't need to try all the variations because the wicket's got a lot of variation anyway, turning more, bouncing higher, all that kind of stuff.

JE: What about the one-day game and the effect it has had on spin bowling? It's tended to dominate cricket over the past five or ten years in England and even more so at international level in Australia since the Packer revolution. In general, the spinner's flight is a lot flatter. How much has that influenced their bowling at Test level?

GM: I think it's definitely had an influence on the way spinners bowl – though it's not so apparent now because players have made decisions between the one-day game and the first-class game and defined their roles. For instance, the best all-purpose cricketer I've seen is Allan Border for the way he's implanted a few extra things in his batting to cope with one-day cricket.

As far as bowling in one-day cricket is concerned, all I think about are 'dot balls' – i.e. balls off which a batsman doesn't get a run. You can get a situation like Australia had when we played India in the World Series Cup finals here last year and needed wickets because we'd only scored 170. But, basically, you're just looking to bowl dot ball, dot ball, dot ball all the time. So it has had an influence.

I think if you're good you should be able to adjust between the two types of game. But the tendency has been to bowl a little flatter and quicker to give the batsman less time and fewer options on where to hit the ball. I don't know whether it's because cricket has changed so much in the past decade or what, but I think spinners definitely bowl quicker now then they did years ago.

JE: That's because spinners are generally looking to attack with more men around the bat. The men at mid on and mid off are more often up than back and you don't see many deep midwickets unless the chap starts to hit you over the top. Before, they used to bowl a lot slower and have their fielders back – and batsmen attacked them. I think it's the attitude in the game that's changed from amateur to professional.

GM: Yeah. I remember being told that Brian Close, playing in his first Test, was caught on the fence for a duck going for it against a spinner. That really blew me up! Yeah, the attitude would definitely be a reason for the change in style. You didn't see many bat–padders around the batsmen but now they're very important.

JE: Let's talk a little bit about wickets. Wickets like the Sydney Cricket Ground. . . .

GM: Love bowling on it!

JE: So do I. But there are not enough wickets like it around in the world at the moment. I say they should be regarded as good cricket wickets. Batsmen can still play shots against bad bowling. And the bowlers have still got to be good to get wickets. When the ball does turn there is less margin for error in the length and the line that you bowl, more balls to hit off the back foot because they stand up a bit higher. I think this match has proved that spinning wickets do produce good cricket.

GM: Yeah – like the last two Shield finals we've had at the SCG.

The wickets weren't real bunsen burners but they definitely turned. And yet a lot of runs were scored.

But it's a fact that batsmen don't play the spinning ball as well as they used to do because there are not so many turning wickets in world cricket these days. Traditionally, Australian batsmen are not supposed to play very well against the seaming or moving ball under English conditions; now a lot of batsmen all round the world seem to struggle with the ball that turns a lot.

I'd certainly like to see more turning wickets. I had one of my biggest disappointments on our tour of India. I was expecting the ball to really turn there but the wickets turned out to be quite flat.

JE: I had exactly the same experience on my first tour there in 1981–2. We lost the first Test in Bombay because of a couple of bad umpiring decisions and I finished up being dropped – on the grounds that we couldn't afford to lose two wickets to bad decisions and needed the extra batsman! After that we played on the flattest wickets of all time and lost the series 1–0. Then on our next Indian tour in 1984–5 (when I didn't go and Phil Edmonds and Pat Pocock helped England win) Graeme Fowler and Mike Gatting both scored double centuries – in the same match.

GM: Outrageous!

JE: The wickets are not what they used to be when India had Bedi, Prasanna, Chandrasekhar and Venkat, and were obviously looking to dominate through spin. Having gone there expecting to bowl on turning wickets, I was very disappointed that we only came across them in the up-country games. And I'm afraid that's pretty general wherever you play.

Still, whatever the wickets are like, it's obviously a help to you being a batsman as well as a bowler because it adds another string to your bow. But do you think your success with the bat in Test cricket may have played a part in undermining people's belief in your spin bowling?

GM: When I first started playing Test cricket, I was a bowler who batted in the context of the team. I was the only spinner in the team, so basically I had been picked to bowl. Yet until then I'd always thought of myself as a batsman who bowled a bit. I hadn't been bowling full on and I'd missed a period between 1977 and 1982 when I didn't do much bowling at all. It was only when I changed grade clubs in Sydney that I bowled for half a season, was picked to play for New South Wales and then had a sharp ride into Test cricket.

I think it has been a problem and it's been disappointing because while I've done OK with the ball, at times I still feel as though I've got a long way to go and it could be a long time before I peak. Certainly I've got a lot more work to do with my bowling. So, to answer your question, yes it has been a downer for me because I was titled as a spin bowler and it has cost me, I think. But, gee, I would hate to believe that I've been *too* successful as a batsman. I'm sure that the people who know the game, and certainly the selectors, would see my batting as a real bonus. I can understand what you're trying to get at, but, my God, the horror if that was true!

JE: Turning to this Test series, Australia performed badly in the first Test at Brisbane and England came through to win with me managing to take five wickets in the second innings. And suddenly everybody was saying that spin was going to dominate the series. But then we came across three wickets at Perth, Adelaide and Melbourne which didn't help the spin bowlers and we finished up just trying to contain the batsmen rather than take wickets. Now we've finally come to Sydney, where it was always going to turn, and you're out of the side. Having played in the earlier matches, how disappointed are you to miss out on playing on your own ground where you would obviously have done a good job, taken a few wickets and made up for what had gone before?

GM: Well, obviously it's very disappointing for me to be left out at Sydney, my home turf, knowing that the wicket was going to help slow bowling. It's definitely easier on a turning wicket where you're allowed more latitude, you can get away with more, basically. What made it worse was that I couldn't remember coming on at any time during the series when the opposition was under any pressure whatsoever.

But the bottom line was not just that I was disappointed but that I'd been disappointing. When I look back to the first Test, I remember dropping Ian Botham before he went on to make 138 and thinking how important it would have been for me to have got off to a good start. Then I had a few screamers dropped off me at Perth, and that kind of thing never helps.

I thought I'd been scoring some pretty good runs during the series and it would have been much more enjoyable playing in front of my own crowd. And there would have been the added bonus of bowling with another spinner. I'd only bowled with Peter Sleep at Adelaide, so that would have been very important as well.

When you bowl with another spinner at the other end, you get a bit of a rapport going, you get through your overs quicker, you put more pressure on the batsmen because you're at 'em more often. I've missed that this series.

JE: So what will you look to do now to try to force your way back into the Test side?

GM: Just to be a little more successful than I've been recently. Even for New South Wales, I haven't done a very good job this season, which has also disappointed me. To get back into the Test team I think I have to do a little more work with my mind, actually – to sit down and think about good things, watch a few videos, fill myself with positive thoughts, remember the good old days, the way it was. Basically it's chin up, shoulders back and tits out!

But, above all, I'm obviously going to have to perform very well in the early games next season. The bloke [Peter Taylor] is going to be in the team and he's going to be bowling in front of me.

JE: Cricket needs personalities – especially in the spin bowling department – and your enthusiasm in the nets and on the field are well known. What is your advice to the budding Greg Matthewses of Australia?

GM: Phew! Good luck!

JE: Yes . . . but in the sense that it takes a lot of dedication and hard work to develop into a Test cricketer?

GM: I'll tell you, that's the bottom line. If I think about scoring a hundred ten times, I think about taking five wickets in an innings once. It's very important to think about it – to prepare yourself for bowling by thinking about taking wickets just as you prepare yourself for batting by thinking about scoring runs. I don't do enough of that. And I think it's very important for kids to do it.

The most important thing in life, I think, is that if you really want to do something and you've got that little bit of talent, then you must go for it. I'm not a great talent or anything like that – in fact I feel really weird talking to you like this! – but I really wanted to play cricket and was fortunate that a few opportunities opened up for me. But the bottom line was that I *wanted* it and I grabbed it . . . well, I've sort of grabbed it on and off. And it was just that 'want'.

You can do a lot of things in life if you really want to do them. You can cite examples of people who have been very ill and recovered from diseases they should have died from; people who can't walk yet manage to live life to the full; and many, many sportsmen and women who have achieved feats against all the odds. 'Want' is the most important thing. So if you want to be a cricketer, and hopefully a spin bowler, get in there, think about it, put the hours in and *do* it.

That conversation will, I hope, give you an insight into the character and personality of one of the most colourful cricketers in the game – and help to explain why I, for one, hope that he can not only force his way back into the Australian Test side but also go on to develop into a top-class off spinner.

I am sure that he can improve on what he has done as a bowler so far – just as I am sure that he would perform much better in another team. Having a good spin bowler at the other end – as I with Phillippe Edmonds – would be of great value to him at international level. For one thing, it would give him someone to whom he could relate and talk.

Matthews loves talking about the game in general and the technique of spin bowling in particular. He even wanted to get into the nets with me to talk about the things I try to do in different situations. It didn't seem to be the right time or place when we were locked in combat on three different fronts, but I hope we will get round to it one day. Meanwhile, I must say I was impressed by the way he came back to bowl in the World Series Cup matches. He didn't fire it in flat but bowled with loop; he had a good line and length; he bowled to his field; and he varied his pace beautifully. As he says, he really wants to do it – and even more so now that he has got something to prove.

If I sympathized with Greg Matthews and the predicament in which he found himself, then I felt even more strongly for Roger Harper. He has so much ability as a very, very good bowler, a more than useful batsman and probably the best fielder in the world that he would walk into any Test side – apart from the West Indies. But as long as they continue to be successful, they are not going to change from the way they have played their cricket for the past ten years – with the emphasis on quick bowlers and an almost continual pace barrage.

It would take a radical change in the nature of the wickets throughout the world to encourage them to include a spinner on a regular basis, and I am afraid that there is little sign of that happening. In the Caribbean itself, wickets are deteriorating to such an extent that even their own cricket is suffering. The young batsmen are simply not coming through because they are at the mercy of the fast bowlers. Test cricket survives because crowds still thrill to the spectacle of the pacemen in full cry – but it is not a particularly healthy environment for a young cricketer like Roger Harper to flourish.

I think it is such a shame because, to me, Roger is the complete cricketer. You can talk about all the other West Indians but none of them has as much all-round talent as Harper. Yet because of the way things are, he is going to play more Test matches away from home than he is in his native Caribbean. In Australia, the West Indies would probably prefer another quick bowler because of the extra pace and bounce in the wickets there. And although he should be fairly certain of touring India, Pakistan and, perhaps, England, he will always need to be batting, bowling and fielding at his peak just to retain his place in the side.

His batting obviously needs a bit of tuning because he is not as consistent as he should be, but he has proved that he has the ability with some big scores in county cricket and in Tests. His fielding is second to none. He has an excellent pair of hands and lightning reflexes anywhere close to the wicket, and in the outfield he is swifter than anybody over the ground and has a magnificent throw.

As for his bowling, his approach is reminiscent of the legendary Lance Gibbs, whose retirement with 309 Test wickets – more than any other spinner in the history of the game – marked the end of an era in West Indian cricket. Roger probably doesn't bowl as wide of the crease or get quite as chest on as Lance did. But, like Gibbs, he is tall, he gets up high to deliver the ball and he has lots of variations with good flight and change of pace. It was only natural, then, that I should begin our talk by asking him:

John Emburey: Lance Gibbs was the last genuine finger spinner to make any real impact for the West Indies. Since he came

from Guyana like yourself, did he influence you in any way or
was becoming an off spinner just a natural thing for you?

Roger Harper: Well, I would say that becoming an off spinner
did come naturally to me – but after my initial interest I sort of
looked on Lance as an idol and saw his achievements as
something to aim for.

JE: Over the past decade, the West Indies have been producing
fast bowler after fast bowler. What made you – tall and athletic
and ideally built to be a fast bowler – want to be a spinner?

RH: I think that when I first started to play cricket, the fast
bowlers were not quite as dominant as they were to become.
Lance was still around and there were a few other spinners on
the fringe of the side. So although fast bowlers played a part in
the West Indies attack, their presence was not quite as
overwhelming as it is today. We didn't have four genuine quick
bowlers in the team then. It was only as I developed and got
into first-class cricket that the fast bowlers came on to the
scene in larger numbers and eventually took over the West
Indies attack.

JE: How hard has that been for you? How frustrating is it sitting
on the sidelines for match after match at home and playing
most of your Test matches overseas?

RH: I couldn't argue about being on the sidelines. The fast
bowlers were winning the matches so I have just had to bide my
time and wait until my chances came.

JE: You mean wait until you came across wickets which looked
as though they might take a bit of spin – or perhaps got on
flatter wickets which might impede the fast bowlers?

RH: Yes – but the trouble with that is that our fast bowlers
have been bowling sides out even on flat wickets. They have
been getting results all the time. That's why the selectors keep
on playing them. I think what has helped me to get into the
team from time to time is that I'm supposed to be able to bat a
bit . . . though you wouldn't have thought so recently!

JE: In view of the situation you found yourself in, did you ever

Three more international batsmen who command the spinners' respect. Gordon Greenidge (top left), who has only just stopped bullying me; Javed Miandad (top right), who comes down the pitch without any early warning; and Sunil Gavaskar (below), who knows all the answers.

Who would be a spinner against this quartet? Ian Botham's awesome power can make you cringe (top left); Mike Gatting treats you with utter disdain (top right); Graham Gooch's attitude is quite imperious, especially against me (below); and as for the eager, young Paul Johnson, I just don't know where to bowl at him (right).

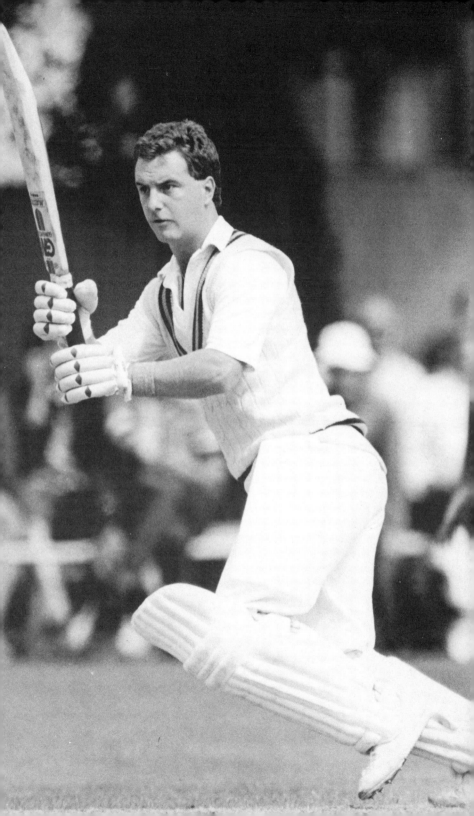

When the ball turns. Phillippe Edmonds (top) leaves the ground in a concerted but unsuccessful appeal against India's Mohammad Azharuddin at Madras, while Pakistan's Abdul Qadir (below) is almost in orbit as he gets the verdict against England's Nick Cook at Karachi.

think about becoming a fast bowler, especially in view of your height and physique?

RH: No. You see I had started playing cricket seriously and bowling spin when I was 13 years old at school – the same age as you, I think – and though I was tall for my age I never thought I would grow to be this big. In any case, I always wanted to be a spinner. It's just what I wanted to do.

JE: And your height is an advantage because you can get a bit of extra bounce and vary your length more easily. But when you are first brought on to bowl – and bearing in mind that you are invariably coming on after a succession of 'strike' bowlers – what is going through your mind? Are you like me, trying to bowl two or three maidens and pitch a few balls on the spot before you start varying it?

RH: Well, when I first started playing first-class cricket for Guyana, our attack was based mainly on spin. We had two fast bowlers – or, more accurately, two medium fast bowlers – and usually two off spinners, myself and another guy, plus a leg spinner. And bowling with other spinners is a lot different from bowling with fast bowlers . . . as I have learned from my experience with the West Indies team.

In a spin-orientated attack, you know that you're going to bowl a long spell, you pace yourself better, you're not trying to get a wicket with every ball. But in the West Indies attack, and particularly when I first got into the team, I tended to think that if I didn't do something pretty soon then I'd be off. There were four other guys waiting to bowl – and they were guys who bowled batsmen out every day, day in, day out. I felt I had to do something just to keep the ball in my hand. That affected my bowling to a certain extent because I was trying to do something every ball, and that's not the way spinners are supposed to bowl really.

You're supposed to settle in, settle down and be prepared to bowl in long spells and work the guy out and set him up and that sort of thing rather than try to bowl him out with every ball. That's the difference between bowling fast and bowling spin. With greater experience, I do now tend to think that I've got to bowl the spinner's way, keeping it as tight as possible and thinking the batsman out – however long it takes me.

JE: I find it difficult bowling in a Test match when I'm the only spinner in the side. How do you find that? Do you feel under pressure when you're the only spinner and the wicket looks as though it might turn?

RH: Yes. I think that I'm automatically expected to bowl the other side out.

JE: This is the thing. Because the wicket looks as though it might turn, they expect you to take wickets all of a sudden with the result that you yourself lose patience and your bowling suffers.

RH: Right. That's exactly it . . . especially when you're beating the bat regularly and you don't get the guy out.

JE: Then you make the mistake of bowling too fast and trying to do too much?

RH: Right. That's just it.

JE: OK then, in that case, do you think that spin bowlers are going to survive the domination of the fast bowlers in Test cricket? And, if they do, what sort of future do you see for them?

RH: I think the spinners are going to come back into their own one day.

JE: Certainly in the World Series Cup one-day internationals we're playing at the moment, the spinners are playing a part. Australia are playing two and they're already in the finals; we've played one and sometimes two; and although your fast bowlers are still dominant you and Viv Richards have both bowled off spin. What sort of role do you see for the spinners now? Will it be more of a defensive, containing job, putting pressure on the batsmen and trying to force them to make mistakes? Or will it be more of a wicket-taking role?

RH: I'm not sure. When I come on to bowl for the West Indies, you can almost hear quite a few of the batsmen saying to themselves: 'Well, OK, we've seen off the fast bowlers . . . now we can relax a bit. Not that we're going to give our wickets away but we are going to play a few more shots.' And certainly in one-day matches they do look to score mainly off me.

But, to try and answer your question, I think so much depends on the strength of your fast bowling attack. If you have a pretty good pace attack, the spinner is going to have to play a more defensive role. If your attack isn't so sharp, I think you have to sort of blend in and be a strike bowler as well.

JE: Obviously most of the kids in the West Indies want to be quick bowlers but there must be one or two young cricketers who would like to bowl spin. In view of your experience, what advice would you give them? What should they concentrate on more than anything else?

RH: You're right. Not everybody in the West Indies wants to bowl fast and there are a few good young spinners around. The most important thing for them to remember about spin bowling is that once they have developed the basic action they must learn to be patient. It's a case of being willing to wait and think batsmen out.

JE: Yes, but will they be allowed to do that? How much effect does the thinking of the captain – in your case Viv Richards – have on the success of a spinner? Or the lack of success?

RH: Well, Viv took over a team in which pace had been doing the job successfully for a number of years and spin had played only a minor role. And I think that's still the case with the West Indies team under Viv. I do think that spin still has a part to play – but not as big a part as the fast bowlers have!

Within minutes of our conversation – on the eve of the one-day international at Devonport in Tasmania where England became the first team ever to knock the West Indies out of the World Series Cup – I heard a whisper that Roger was going to be dropped from the party to tour New Zealand. I could hardly believe it at the time but it was confirmed a couple of days later.

The news came as quite a shock. His track record in Test and international cricket was not the greatest – and his replacement, fellow Guyana off spinner Clyde Butts, had apparently been more successful on their tour of Pakistan. But one wondered just who in the West Indian hierarchy disliked Roger Harper.

He had not had a particularly good one-day series with the bat but he had bowled tidily enough and, as ever, fielded quite superbly. And with the West Indies going to a place like New Zealand with so many of their fast bowlers suddenly seeming susceptible to injury (indeed Michael Holding had announced his retirement from Test cricket by the end of the first Test) they could have done with two spinners in the squad. It wouldn't have mattered that they were both off spinners. England have toured both Australia and the West Indies with three off spinners in the past so I do not see why the West Indies could not have taken two.

I was disappointed to see such a talented cricketer as Roger Harper being treated in this way – although I was obviously not as disappointed as he was. All he could do was pack his bags, go home to the Caribbean, have a couple of months off and then get back into it with Guyana before returning to Northamptonshire where he was eventually to lose his place in county cricket to West Indian fast bowlers Winston Davis and Curtly Ambrose.

Roger's first priority, however, should have been to arrange a meeting with Viv Richards and the selectors and find out just what he had to do to cement his place in the West Indies team. At 23, he was still young enough to develop into a world-class bowler and go on to captain the West Indies, which had always seemed to be his destiny. After all, when I was 23 I had not even made my first-class debut.

However, he also had to give his bowling some serious

thought. He seemed to have developed something of a one-day mentality and had to get his mind more attuned to playing over three, four and five days. And that was not going to be easy after playing in so many limited-overs matches in which the spinner gets into the habit of bowling much flatter, firing in quick balls to force the batsman on to the back foot in the hope that he will hit them straight at the fielders.

It was very noticeable when we were in Australia that Peter Taylor, having made such a remarkable entry into Test cricket with only half-a-dozen first-class matches behind him, was still looping the ball in exactly the same way in the one-dayers. One could not help wondering how much his bowling would be affected if he continued in international cricket and found himself bowling on rather less generous wickets than he was used to at Sydney.

Taylor's testing time was still to come. Harper's was upon him – and he had to move in the opposite direction and get back to bowling like off spinners are supposed to bowl. But, after talking to him, I was sure that he knew that.

A Different Turn

THROUGHOUT THIS BOOK, one name – that of my long-time
Middlesex and England spin bowling partner Phillippe Henri
Edmonds – has kept cropping up, sometimes, you may think, in
a derogatory way but mostly, I sincerely hope, in complimen-
tary terms.

For let me make one thing perfectly clear. I consider myself
very lucky to have arrived at the same club round about the
same time as him because we have been able to feed off each
other, to our mutual benefit, throughout our careers.

It is not often that one county has two Test-class spin
bowlers on its staff at the same time. In fact only the
partnerships of Jim Laker and Tony Lock at Surrey, John
Mortimore and David Allen at Gloucestershire and the Yorkshire pairings of Johnny Wardle and Bob Appleyard, and Don
Wilson and Ray Illingworth, spring readily to mind. I am sure
that it was as good for them as it has been for Phillippe and me.
The competition has motivated both of us. And the pressure
we have been been able to exert on batsmen from both ends of
the pitch has made each of us more successful.

We have very little in common as individuals. I come from a
working-class background in South London and progressed
through what you might call the normal channels – school,
youth, club and 2nd XI – before getting into county cricket.

Phillippe, born and brought up in Zambia (then Northern
Rhodesia) of an English father and a Belgian mother, went
straight from school at Cranbrook into the first-class game in

his first year at Cambridge, which is a marvellous way to start a cricket career.

That privileged upbringing was where I began a conversation with him which should give you the essential flavour of a contrary individual who in the days before Margaret Thatcher became Prime Minister was nicknamed 'Maggie' in the Middlesex dressing room – because, whatever anyone said about any topic under discussion, he was always the leader of the opposition.

I will make no further comment on our wide-ranging discussion, apart from pointing out that we talked in the dressing room at Old Trafford while Middlesex were batting in a championship match against Lancashire, and that the rest of the team was listening – and chipping in at times. And Phillippe's reply to my very first question should not be taken out of context. It was very much tongue in cheek, purely designed to capture the attention of his five West Indian-born colleagues and typical of his mischievous and highly individualistic sense of humour. It was greeted, I hasten to add, with peals of laughter!

John Emburey: How much effect did being born in Zambia, growing up and playing your early cricket there, have on your career?
Phillippe Edmonds: Being born in Zambia had a tremendous influence on me. Being brought up in the black man's environment gave me an innate sense of superiority which, of course, is a very positive, beneficial, psychological aspect when it flows on to the cricket field. Being positive and feeling superior and dominating the batsman is very important. I play at Middlesex where we've got five of these fellows and therefore that feeling is reinforced.
JE: No, seriously . . . did you have any coaching as a youngster in Zambia?
PE: None at all. No.

JE: And when you came to England and went to school at Cranbrook and then went up to Cambridge, did everything just come naturally? Did you bowl seam before you bowled spin or did you go straight into it as a left arm spinner?

PE: I bowled seam until I was about 14, I suppose, and I think that's quite important really as a youngster inasmuch as I reckon that you need a strong body action to bowl spin. If you look at the likes of Fred Titmus and Ray Illingworth and yourself, I gather, a lot of guys bowled seam first of all and then converted to spin.

I think it's a common mistake that a lot of schoolteachers make when a kid of about eight or nine comes up and says: 'I want to be a spinner.' I think that's a lot of rubbish. They've just got to learn to bowl and bowl and bowl and develop their actions.

JE: Do you think you were a much more natural cricketer when you were at Cambridge than after you became a professional cricketer?

PE: No, I don't think that. But I know what happened. In Zambia we only had one school which did A levels, so that school had to play its cricket in the adult league in Lusaka. And in the late Fifties and early Sixties it was a very good standard of cricket. There were a lot of guys from Rhodesia and South Africa who came up to the copper belt on contract, guys who had played top quality club cricket, which meant that for schoolboys the majority of our players were quite mature cricketers.

The very big difference when I came to school in England was that it was schoolboy cricket as opposed to adult cricket and I did very little, basically because I was so frustrated with the guys I was playing with. In fact I did sweet fanny adams. Then I got up to Cambridge where there were players of the calibre of Majid Khan and Dudley Owen-Thomas and quite a few more very good cricketers. And obviously we had the privilege of playing county cricket.

I think I played some of my best cricket in my first year at Cambridge. My thinking was all very positive. Not having experienced or even watched any county cricket at all, I couldn't believe that some of the guys I was playing against were actually professional cricketers earning their living. I would just come on and bowl and I took it for granted that I was going to bowl well.

JE: Would that have been under the captaincy of Majid?

PE: Yes, for the first two years.

JE: So do you think Majid had a big influence on your career, at least on your thinking about the game at that early stage?

PE: Yes . . . inasmuch as he reinforced the aspect of being positive and playing the game. And, because he was a world-class player himself, one tended to compare all batsmen with him and when they failed to reach his high standards one tended to think they were very ordinary players and therefore one would think very positively as a bowler. Just that.

JE: You played your first Test match in 1975, only two years after coming down from Cambridge. Do you think much has changed since then? Your ability? Your attitude? As you get older, is your arm coming over slower? Or do you think there isn't much difference?

PE: I think I'm probably a more, er, responsible bowler than I used to be.

JE: You're talking to us, remember, Henri!

PE: No, no – I think I'm probably a little bit meaner than I used to be in Test cricket. I bowl more maidens than I used to do.

JE: How many overseas tours have you been on?

PE: Certainly not enough! Four, I think it is.

JE: Do you find bowling overseas more enjoyable than bowling in England because the wickets are harder with more bounce?

PE: No, not especially. I think that's a bit of a myth.

JE: Oh. Well, I prefer bowling overseas because of that.

PE: Do you? I find that wickets the world over are very much the same. We went to India and played on wickets that were slow and low, and I can't say the wickets in Australia on our last tour were dramatically different from those in England when the Australians were last over playing us. I don't think they were much harder.

JE: In that case, how significant was the performance of the England spinners in that Ashes series in 1986–7?

PE: Well, to my mind, I think the most significant aspect of the series was the bowling of Graham Dilley. I thought he was the fulcrum of our attack because he was making the initial breakthrough for us. He was getting out the top-line players, which, inevitably, put them on the defensive because they were chasing 450 a time and they quite often started with two wickets down. With regard to the spinners, I thought we did extremely well by holding positions for long periods of time, allowing the captain room and flexibility to think. . . .

Mike Gatting: Very good – I agree with that entirely.

PE: . . . because we were able to control and dominate what was happening on the field for long periods. That happened at Brisbane, it happened at Perth, it happened at Adelaide. And I think it's been the pattern of our English cricket over the past three or four years when the spinners have actually done a lot of bowling. It certainly happened in India when Pat Pocock and I bowled a lot, it happened in the home series against the Aussies in 1985 and I think it's been pretty healthy for English cricket. I know you get the purists who say that Edmonds and Emburey don't take enough wickets and maybe they're right in that. . . .

JE: But do you think we're used in the role of wicket-taking bowlers or that of containing bowlers? There has been a big theory among past England captains that it's a fast bowlers' game, but I think we still bowl to get wickets.

We've always been fairly mean in our bowling, anyway, we've never really been smashed around, but we're still trying to get batsmen out.

PE: All I know is that Test matches are five-day matches and they're long, long matches. If you can control what's happening on the field then, by and large, you're on top.

JE: Whether it's the spinners getting the wickets or the seamers getting the wickets, the whole objective is to win the game.

PE: Yes. But if you're controlling what's happening in the field, not only taking wickets but controlling positions, then, generally speaking, you'll come out on top. I think that's what happened when you and I have been bowling over the past two or three series.

JE: How important do you find it bowling in tandem with another spinner? Do you find it's a lot easier to bowl with another spinner at the other end or do you find it doesn't bother you?

PE: I think rhythm is very important and I like to have the ball in my hands a lot of the time. So, when I'm bowling with you and you're taking two minutes to bowl an over and I'm taking two minutes to bowl an over, the ball is in my hands a lot. And, by and large, you're quite a mean bowler and we can develop pressure. The momentum is there for over after over and you can feel the pressure mounting up on the batsmen. I think we work very well together in this way.

JE: The great thing about bowling long spells and getting into a rhythm is that although we may not have been taking wickets, we automatically fall into that rhythm in the next game without having to look for it. There were a lot of occasions back in 1977 and 1978 when we bowled long spells together and it was much, much easier to keep the momentum going.

PE: Yes, that's the natural consequence of bowling a lot. But I'm not sure that answers the question about bowling in tandem. What I find about bowling with you is that we get a nice rhythm going together, and the pressure is on the batsmen all the time because the overs are ticking by quickly and quite often they feel they've got to get on with it. But they're apprehensive about playing shots, and things start to go well from our point of view. I think this happens quite a lot.

JE: Right. Now, we've got the captain of England eavesdropping here. Do you find it a lot easier playing in a Test match with two spinners in the side or just the one?

PE: I've never played as the only spinner in the side!

MG: Ha, ha, ha.

JE: So when you've played your Test matches there have always been two spinners?

PE: Er . . . by and large. I think probably the only time I played as a single spinner was when you broke your nose in 1986. And I bowled extremely well, I recall. Four wickets against New Zealand at Lord's, if memory serves me right.

JE: Yes . . . I was disappointed not to be playing because it turned.

PE: No it didn't – it was flight and guile!

JE: OK. Now, apart from the obvious difference between us of you being a left arm spin bowler and me being a right arm spin bowler, do you think that one has an obvious advantage over the other?

PE: No, I can't say that. But I must say I do enjoy bowling at left handers because I enjoy turning the ball into the stumps – particularly in Test matches when from my point of view there is inevitably a bit of rough outside the left hander's off stump. I usually find it quite encouraging bowling at the likes of Allan Border. I also find that there's more margin for error when I'm bowling to left handers, and that makes it slightly easier.

JE: But don't you find it frustrating when you are actually beating the bat and the ball is continually hitting the pads, when it's easy for the batsmen to play with the bat away from the pad and virtually kick the ball away?

PE: Well, I'm not sure that it is. Obviously if the ball is turning quite substantially I think that, psychologically, it's more devastating to get the ball turning away from the bat.

JE: So don't you think it creates more of a panic feeling in the

batsman when the ball is actually beating the bat and going into
the wicketkeeper's hands or something?

PE: I don't know. I think that depends on the batsman. Talking
to people like the late Kenny Barrington, I think he far
preferred playing left armers than he did off spinners. I think
there were two or three players of that ilk, really top-class
players, who preferred playing the ball leaving the bat than the
ball moving into them.

From my viewpoint, on turning wickets I find it a lot more
encouraging bowling to right handers; on flat wickets I find it a
lot easier in many ways bowling to left handers.

JE: Yes, I tend to agree with that. On flat wickets it is easier to
bowl with the ball going into the batsman.

PE: I also find it less of a strain bowling over the wicket than I
do bowling round the wicket.

JE: How important do you find that aspect – bowling over or
round the wicket? You do most of your bowling round the
wicket because the majority of the batsmen happen to be right
handers. And you very rarely bowl over the wicket to right-
handed batsmen. Is there a reason for this?

PE: Well, I think it's tradition more than anything else. I'm sure
I don't bowl over the wicket enough to right handers. But I
think there's a psychological block among our umpires who
would not conceive of giving me an lbw decision bowling over
the wicket at a right-handed batter. And I think it's totally
wrong.

JE: I can't wholly agree with you there. You do get a lot of drift,
you make the ball curve in the air, so if you are bowling over the
wicket to a right hander you're doing exactly the same as a left
arm seamer bowling inswing, especially if the ball doesn't turn.

PE: That's right. But, in my opinion, and I'm sure Paul
Downton, our wicketkeeper, will confirm it, the idea of an
umpire giving out a batter lbw with me bowling left arm over is
negligible. I don't think I've ever experienced it.

Paul Downton: I don't think that's true. If you bowl over the wicket, which you do very rarely, you've got a chance. Bowling round, you've got no chance at all.

PE: There's an idea in this country that left arm spin bowlers only bowl over the wicket because they want to bowl into the rough outside leg stump. That goes not only for our umpires but for the Press, the chairman of selectors, everybody. That is reinforced by the fact that we actually do bowl left arm over into the rough outside leg stump. But *every time* they see it, they say 'Oh, he must be bowling left arm over into the rough', and that is often a load of rubbish.

PD: I don't know whether I can go along with all this. It depends on the situation.

JE: I can't go all the way with it, either. Perhaps it just applies to left armers. I find it easier bowling over the wicket rather than round the wicket to a left hander like Allan Border, and there's a lot less rough outside his leg stump.

PE: I'm sure you're right. But you misunderstand what I'm saying. What I'm saying is that left arm spinners should bowl over the wicket a lot more than they do, bowling on to middle and leg and looking to hit the stumps so that if the ball does drift a bit you get 'em out lbw. But the fact is that we don't do that, and it's partly because tradition dictates that we don't and partly because umpires don't give lbw's on the grounds that they think we are bowling outside leg stump. The combination of these things amounts to left armers bowling round the wicket all the time.

But the older I get the more I believe that the old stagers, the old codgers have been right in saying that the left armer should bowl round the wicket, toss the ball up wide of the off stump to a six-three offside field and get the batsman driving. And I think that on many occasions I've been far too attacking in my attitude, anticipating getting bat–pad catches with a man close in on either side mainly because there have been a lot of half-chances and you keep thinking that one of them is go-ing to be converted into a wicket. Then you look at the end

of the day and you've bowled 30 overs for very little reward.
JE: Let's talk a little bit about the problems that can affect a
spin bowler, the pressure that you and the people around you
are under when things go wrong and how you overcome these
things.

There was a time round about 1979 when you had an injury
to your knee and over the years you have had a recurring back
problem. And you went through a period when you were
unable to pitch the ball where you wanted to pitch the ball. Did
your confidence go then? Or was it just a matter of time before
everything came back?
PE: Obviously the mind is a very strange thing and plays very
strange tricks. And I have struggled in two periods, really. One
was that time you refer to when I did not know where the ball
was pitching at all and in fact reached the stage where it was
difficult to let it go.

The second time was when we toured India in 1984–5 when
I found it impossible to run up to the wicket for no known
reason. I just found it absolutely impossible.
PD: It was extraordinary looking from the other end – just
watching him trying to start his run.
JE: It does seem that when something like that does go wrong
and the spinner loses it, for some reason it happens to left
armers far more than off spinners. In recent years, it has
happened to you, Fred Swarbrook at Derbyshire and John
Childs at Gloucestershire, although he has got it back at Essex.
I wonder why it happens to one particular type of bowler.
PE: It might be an interesting phenomenon to research. Maybe
there is some psychological combination to bowling left arm
round the wicket. It is a fact that these problems do seem to
affect left armers and not off spinners.

I cannot really talk about it in that context any more. But,
with regard to me, I think what happened when I was really
struggling to pitch the ball was that I had a period of intense
aggravation with Mike Brearley. This is only an hypothesis,

right. But there was a period of time when Ian Gould christened me 'Chanel No 5' because I was fifth choice bowler. Whereas I had always regarded myself as the first change bowler after the seamers, I ended up being fifth change. . . .
JE: It was not fifth change – it was third change.
PE: All right – but fifth bowler who was only sort of tolerated as a bowler. And there were often situations where I felt I should have been bowling and I wasn't bowling. Then, when I was eventually brought on to bowl, I perhaps tried a bit too hard and that caused me aggro.
JE: Didn't this mostly happen at Lord's rather than in away games? Wasn't it because we had someone like Mike Selvey who could bowl long spells at the end that was preferred for you, while Wayne Daniel would bowl a shorter spell followed by another seamer and then, perhaps, myself. Or did you feel you were being put under pressure by Brearley?
PE: I don't know about that. I am just trying to rationalize it. Mine is only a subjective analysis and I might be totally wrong. But I think what happened was that over a period of time my confidence was eroded to such a stage where I didn't really want to bowl. And then when I did come on to bowl I was trying too hard and things didn't work out.

Fortunately, though, after a two-week spell or whatever, I went and played for the second team and bowled lots and lots of overs in the middle and gradually got it back. I think there's no substitute for getting in the middle and actually bowling.
JE: I agree with that entirely. Now, what do you think of the more general problem in this country? Why are there so few young spin bowlers coming through into the first-class game?
PE: I don't know.
JE: Do you think the reintroduction of uncovered wickets is going to make any difference?
PE: I just don't know. I haven't played much club cricket but the cricket I have played on club wickets has always been on wickets that must be responsive to spin. . . .

JE: Soft and puddingy.

PE: . . . and I cannot believe that a good spin bowler in club cricket is not going to wreak havoc. So I'm at a loss to understand why there aren't any bowlers who bowl spin in club cricket. You cannot expect there to be bowlers in first-class cricket if there aren't any in club cricket.

JE: Well, there probably are spin bowlers in club cricket but they're mainly older players, and I'm talking about the younger element, the school-leaver. I know it is early days for them and they may not have the ability at that age. But the two young boys we have got on the Middlesex staff, Jamie Sykes and Phillip Tufnell, are 21 and 20 respectively and so far they haven't fulfilled our hopes for them. They have still got plenty of time, of course, but at what stage do you start worrying that they're not going to make it?

PE: I don't know. I've absolutely no idea.

JE: Then why does it seem to take such a long time? A lot of people say that spinners don't mature until they're 30. Do you think that's a fallacy?

PE: Well, I think one's career goes in stages. It's not a straight line of development. It's much more of a step-by-step development. You step up a rung and then there's a plateau and you step up another rung and then there's another plateau.

I reckon that, psychologically, I was as strong as I've ever been when I played my first year in county cricket at Cambridge University.

I had absolutely no knowledge of the players I was playing against and all I thought was that I was a top-class bowler myself and that I could get anybody out. At the end of the year, though, the players that I had been playing against and who I had thought of as very ordinary players had got 1,500 runs, so it began to sink in that these guys could play. And I think that with experience you realize that not every ball is going to turn, that you are not going to get the guys out all the time.

So gradually, as time goes on, you become a little bit more

reticent psychologically, a little bit more fragile, while counter-balancing that, obviously, is the experience that you have gained of bowling on all sorts of wickets. Right?

JE: Right. Now I'm going to throw the discussion open and bring some of the others in. Why do they think that spinners are not coming through into the game?

Simon Hughes had already mentioned to me about kids playing only 20 overs-a-side matches in the evenings or on Saturday mornings, so spinners don't get the chance to develop because they are not given the opportunity to bowl on the grounds that they are going to get slogged. Are there any other views?

Mike Gatting: I think there are two reasons why spinners are not coming through. One is the fact that they are now playing limited overs in club cricket. The other is that coaches, generally, tend to categorize boys and encourage them to bowl seamers because it's very difficult for them to bowl spinners at a very young age. And it does take a certain mentality, a different mentality, to be a spin bowler.

In fact, you have to be a very, very strong character to be a spin bowler, I think. And that is another major reason why there are not that many of them about at the moment.

JE: The success of a spin bowler depends to a large extent on the captain and his willingness to bowl him. At school and club level, the games are that much shorter and the captains are probably inexperienced themselves, so they are not going to give the young spin bowler the opportunity.

MG: I don't think there are that many coaches about who actually take an interest in spin bowling, either.

JE: I think Phillippe was right when he talked earlier about kids developing as medium pacers to get the basic action right to start with and then becoming spinners as their hands and fingers get bigger and they can manipulate the ball.

Roland Butcher: My view is that, basically, kids are cast in a role far too early in life – and I'm not just talking about spin bowlers. When I was a young player, not only in Barbados where I grew up but after I came to England as well, I was asked to do everything – to bat, to bowl quick, to bowl medium pace, to bowl spin, to keep wicket. Now I find that kids are told at a very early age: 'You be a batsman, you be a quick bowler, you be a spin bowler, you be a wicketkeeper.' And I think that's wrong.

In my case, when I first went to Lord's, I started off as a leg spinner and only later developed into a batsman. And I believe I was only able to do that because I'd been given the opportunity to do all those other things as a kid. I think this is very important. Kids should not be told what they are going to do but encouraged to do everything until they become comfortable in a particular role and then settle into that.

If you've got a team of Under-10s or whatever, you should try to make sure that those kids do everything – they all bat, they all bowl, they all keep wicket – because you can never know which way they are going to go in the future. In time you may find that bowlers will become batsmen, and vice versa, but they can only do that if they've been encouraged properly at an early age.

JE: Interesting. It would also make it a lot easier when they did reach the top level and they could all bowl in the nets instead of just hanging around if they're purely batsmen who have had their knock.

Right. One more question for Phillippe. You will be 36 this year. Knowing that there are hardly any young spinners coming through to put pressure on you and me, how long do you think you will go on playing Test cricket?

PE: That depends on how flexible the captain of England and the chairman of selectors are!

If they adopt the attitude that I can play as an amateur, I would like to play as long as possible. The probability is that I'm not going to be available to tour ad infinitum. Right? Therefore

I think it's a question of how the powers-that-be look at selecting Test match teams on a domestic basis.

If they are going to keep looking towards the future and planning for tours and so on, then obviously they are not going to pick a side at home on a one-off basis. But I'm a great believer in picking the best team you have available for each particular match.

I can't speak for Mike Gatting and Peter May!

Neither can I. All I can say is that it was absolutely typical of my long-time partner Phillippe Henri Edmonds that he should have wanted to be the first 'player' to become a 'gentleman' since the distinction between the two was abolished in 1962. And the fact that neither Middlesex nor anybody else took him up on his offer was in my view more of a loss to English cricket than people realized.

I was surprised that one or two of the southern counties didn't sound him out about playing for them on a part-time basis as Imran Khan was doing for Sussex. Had this happened, he would surely have done enough bowling to remain in contention for a place in the England side.

It was well enough known that people like Peter May and Fred Titmus did not like his antics – and I must admit that sometimes I was not too keen on them either. But the fact remained that he was still a very good cricketer. And if you were thinking about picking a left arm spinner to play for England, you had to think about Phillippe Henri Edmonds before you thought of anyone else.

Calling All Spinners

WE CAME TO the end of the 1988 season with English cricket in
a state of crisis. Our batting had once again been torn apart by
the West Indian fast bowlers, our own pacemen had once again
been plagued by a succession of injuries – and, worst of all from
my point of view – our spinners had all but disappeared from
the international scene.

There was no shortage of batting talent. Graham Gooch and
Ian Botham were adamant that they had made their last major
tours, Mike Gatting was following David Gower's example and
taking a winter off after his traumatic experiences at home and
abroad, and Chris Broad, Tim Robinson and Bill Athey had all
fallen out of favour. But Tim Curtis was being given the chance
to establish himself as a Test opener, Matthew Maynard had
emerged as a dazzling strokeplayer, and young men like
Michael Atherton and Mark Ramprakash, not to mention that
Zimbabwean genius Graeme Hick, who was due to become
qualified for England in 1991, suggested that we should not be
short of runs in the future.

On the bowling front, Botham had gone into decline even
before his serious spinal operation, Graham Dilley, Neil Foster,
Gladstone Small and Paul Jarvis were all dogged by injuries,
and Phillip DeFreitas was not progressing as smoothly as we all
hoped he would. Yet Richard Ellison, Greg Thomas and
Norman Cowans had all forced themselves back into contention, and with David Lawrence, Jon Agnew, Neil Williams and
Angus Fraser improving all the time, we were not that short of
resources.

I only wish I could have said the same about the spin bowling department, which reflected only too accurately the sad decline in recent years. Phillippe Edmonds had effectively retired at 37 – the same age as his replacement as England's left arm spinner, John Childs. I was 36 and Vic Marks and Nick Cook, the two men who had already been given their chance to replace Phil and me, were 33 and 32 respectively.

Of the other established England-qualified spin bowlers in county cricket, Norman Gifford was 48, Jack Simmons 47, Eddie Hemmings 39, Peter Willey 38, Phil Carrick 36, Geoff Miller, David Graveney and Nigel Cowley all 35, and Rodney Ontong 33.

Now I know that I have already said that spinners do not reach their peak until their early thirties, but I found the situation frightening. Only one relatively young spinner – Worcester's 25-year-old Yorkshire-born slow left arm bowler Richard Illingworth – had appeared with any regularity in county cricket, and he did not really turn the ball very much but just darted it in around middle and leg. Of the rest, Peter Such, a tall off spinner for whom there had been great hopes, had obviously not come up to Nottinghamshire's expectations because they had released him to join Leicestershire where his chances were even more limited because of their reliance on seam. As for Keith Medlycott, another left armer from South London, the Surrey players told me that while he had all the makings of a useful, all-round cricketer, he was not a great spinner of the ball, either.

In fact, as I looked around the counties, I felt that the most interesting proposition might be Ian Folley – especially as he had started out as a left arm seam bowler and been converted to spin by Lancashire. I hoped that it might prove to be a sign of the times, and that if the switch proved to be successful for Ian it might encourage other young seamers to do the same. There were quite enough of them to be going on with!

Such a switch had been made before, of course. I did it

myself, although I was only about 14 at the time. And I think it is probably easier to do it at a later stage in your development, by which time you have learned the basis of bowling at first-class level, which, as I cannot stress too much, is pitching the ball up and keeping it fairly straight.

After that it is just a question of the way you grip the ball in your fingers, with the hand alongside the ball rather than behind it and the wrist cocked – and bowling about 10 yards slower. If it doesn't feel quite right, you can even start off by throwing the ball until you get the rhythm of the wrist and fingers co-ordinated and then come through with the same basic bowling action that you used as a seamer.

If you want an example of a professional who has made the conversion successfully, look at Peter Willey, the Leicester and former Northants all-rounder who was very close to yet another England recall against the West Indies in 1988. 'Will' had to give up bowling seamers because he suffered so much from knee trouble, but he managed to turn himself into a very useful off spinner. He always had a good sideways-on-action and he had no trouble changing his grip and slowing down his pace.

Similarly, Ian Folley was beginning to look the part. I had seen him take wickets against Middlesex at Liverpool and at Lord's and was quite impressed with him. He gave the ball a nice loop and all he seemed to be lacking was a little bit of control and, I would suggest, confidence. I hoped that he would get that from captain David Hughes and coach Alan Ormrod and that he would not be influenced to try to fill the role of 'Flat Jack' Simmons, who has done a magnificent job for Lancashire over the years but is not necessarily a good example for the young spin bowler. Rather than being asked to bowl flat in the style that gave Jack his nickname, Ian had to be encouraged to make use of his undoubted ability to spin the ball.

My major worry on Folley's behalf was that he only seemed

to get into the side when they expected the ball to turn. You would see that he had taken wickets on a turning pitch and won a game for them and then discover that he had been left out of the very next match because there was a bit of grass on the wicket and they were only playing one spinner, in which case it had to be Jack. The same kind of thing was even happening to John Childs and Nick Cook, who was left out of the Northants side on the very weekend that he was picked to play for England.

I think that attitude towards the spinner – and especially the young spinner – is totally wrong. The only way he is ever going to learn to bowl properly is by bowling long spells on good wickets. It's no good only playing him when the right wicket comes along and then saying that he should be in the England team. All of a sudden he would find himself bowling on the flattest wicket he had ever seen in his life and not know where to put the ball.

Elsewhere, everyone with the game of cricket at heart should have been thinking seriously about why there was such a shortage of young spin bowlers coming into county cricket. I have given it a lot of thought myself and have come to the conclusion that there are three basic factors behind the crisis – the general state of wickets, the influence of one-day cricket and the attitude of captains.

Wickets – bad wickets – are undoubtedly the biggest problem in English cricket. Too many counties, desperate for success, are preparing them, or rather *under*-preparing them, to produce results at any cost, and it is not doing anybody any good. There are going to be no winners in the end.

With plenty of grass left on to provide bounce, pace and sideways as well as up and down movement, our leading batsmen are just not getting the opportunity to play the long innings so necessary to build up their confidence for Test cricket, while the younger ones are having to battle simply to survive in the game; average seam bowlers are returning figures that not only exaggerate their ability but are totally irrelevant to the needs of the England team; and the poor old spinner is hardly getting a look-in.

Now I know why the counties are doing it. But their argument that spectators were not coming through the turn-stiles because the England team were doing so badly was a false one. The main reason why England were doing so badly was because those same counties were letting their captains and cricket committees dictate to their groundsmen what kind of wickets they should produce. It was false economy, too. However much more revenue those 'result wickets' generated, I would bet that it did not equal their share of the Test match receipts they received from the Test and County Cricket Board.

To quote Phillippe Edmonds again: 'We are just encourag-ing mediocrity' – and the time has come to do something about it. One way would be for the home side to forfeit the toss and let the visiting captain decide who bats first, but that would be taking away some of the 'glorious uncertainty' that gives the game its appeal.

Another idea would be to have a panel of pitch examiners going around the first-class grounds looking at the wickets and the state of the square and imposing fines if they were not up to standard. But I doubt if that would be any great deterrent. Some clubs would simply look to their sponsors to pay the fines – just as they did when they were fined for falling behind with their over-rates.

My solution would be to hit offending counties where it hurts most – by deducting championship points for sub-standard wickets. Umpires, the most impartial judges of all, are in the best position to assess the condition of wickets, and I don't think it would be asking too much of them to give each wicket a mark out of ten in their normal match report, a poor wicket getting one, two or three, a good wicket eight, nine or ten. If the mark was five, a county would lose five points, if it was four they would lose six points, and so on. But if the mark was over five, they would gain points – one for a mark of six, two for seven, etc. That way counties would be penalized for preparing bad wickets and rewarded for preparing good ones.

I am sure that would go a long way to solving the problem in county cricket – though Test wickets are a different matter. Most of them start off damp these days, and though in principle that should really encourage captains to get their spinners on early to see if the ball will turn, they still prefer to use their faster bowlers and medium pacers who can make it swing and cut.

To my mind, there are two reasons for this sorry state of affairs. One is that a lot of Test wickets have simply been used too much, with the result that they have become so docile that they often have to be given a good soaking to get any life out of them at all. The answer is to follow the example of Surrey, whose groundsman, Harry Brind, took the bold step of digging up and relaying large sections of the ancient Oval square. As a consequence, the Oval is now blessed with good, fast, bouncy wickets which help the quick bowlers and the spinners alike. That can only be good for the game.

The other reason – and I find this infinitely more depressing – is that too many groundsmen seem to think that it is a poor reflection on their ability if a wicket turns at all, and almost a matter for suicide if it looks like breaking up before the end of a match. So they tend to over-compensate by producing wickets which in many cases finish up in the kind of condition they should have been in at the start. It affects the spinner most because the wicket is often at its best for batting at the very time that he is supposed to be turning the ball and trying to force a result. No matter so many matches finish in draws – unless we happen to be playing the West Indies!

I may be asking for the moon but, to me, a good cricket wicket is one which starts dry but helps the quick bowlers early on because of its pace, settles down to give the good batsmen full value for their strokes because the ball is still coming on to the bat, and then begins to turn more and more to afford the spinners their opportunity over the final two days.

At the moment, the spinners are not being given much chance at all – although I thought there was a glimmer of hope for us in 1987 when the Test and County Cricket Board decided to revert to uncovered wickets in the County Championship. This brought an outcry from many captains and players who felt that it would only encourage more negative cricket with sides looking to win the toss, bat first and get as many runs on the board as they could before the weather had a chance to take a hand. There was also the genuine fear that it might affect the prospects of the England side whose playing would have to contend with uncovered wickets while the tourists were preparing on covered ones.

Yet I felt that it was a step in the right direction – albeit a totally opposite direction to the one I have been advocating! All the great spinners of the past played on uncovered wickets. And with the weather affecting bowlers' run-ups as well as the pitches themselves, spinners did most of the bowling – and, naturally enough, took most of the wickets.

Sadly, from my point of view, the experiment with uncovered wickets was abandoned after one season instead of giving it two or three years to see how it worked, and the Test and County Cricket Board introduced four-day cricket to the County Championship for the first time. Again it was on a trial basis, with three four-day games at the start of the season and three more at the end, and again I was in favour of the general idea. But I would have liked to have seen it given a proper trial with a full championship programme of 16 four-day matches.

Unfortunately four-day cricket in England got off to an uncertain start and it was wholly due to the state of the wickets. I cannot emphasize too strongly the need for wickets to be dry at the start of a match, which should not be impossible despite our climate. And if you want to know why, I can do no better than cite the example of Pakistan, where they have the driest wickets I have ever come across.

They not only assist the finger spinner but the leg spinner as well – and it is no coincidence that Pakistan have produced the most exciting and successful spin bowler in the world today in Abdul Qadir.

When I've been in the Middlesex nets at Lord's or at Finchley, I have been struck by the number of youngsters who turn up wanting to bowl spin. A lot of them are too young because their hands and fingers haven't really developed enough to allow them to grip the ball properly. But what is noticeable is that when they run up and bowl, they let the ball go out of the back of the hand because it is more natural to them, and I think we should be doing more to encourage the development of leg spin.

We see very few leg-spinners in English cricket. Sussex did introduce one in Andy Clarke in 1988, though, ironically, he was more successful in one-day cricket than first-class matches. Lancashire and Cambridge University batsman Michael Atherton bowls his leg breaks and googlies quite well and should do so more often, as should Derbyshire captain Kim Barnett, whose case for England selection would have been stronger, in my opinion, if he had not concentrated so hard on his batting to the detriment of his bowling.

Generally speaking, however, our wickets are very much against them, and it was significant that even the great Abdul Qadir did not have that much success in England in 1987 until he got to the final Test at the Oval and a pitch with that vital ingredient – bounce. Then he took 10 of his 11 wickets in the series, seven of them in the first innings, and put England under tremendous pressure when we followed on.

Abdul is a great bowler anywhere, of course, but it is in Pakistan that he really comes into his own. I dare say that it has a little bit to do with Pakistani umpires, who are usually prepared to give batsmen out to the one he pushes through even if it is not necessarily straight, but it is mainly because of his variations and absolute control. The man is just brilliant.

Obviously the most difficult thing is to pick his googly. The more you bat against him, the easier it becomes, and I found that I could actually 'read' it after a while. But as Graham Gooch observed: 'Reading him is one thing but you've still got to play the ball!' What he meant was that you still have to cope with the flight and bounce and degree of turn, which means that even if you can read him it remains as difficult as playing a finger spinner on a turning wicket.

You cannot take liberties by charging down the wicket against him, either. I'll never forget the way he bowled against us in the 1987 World Cup. He not only changed the pace of his bowling but mixed it up with leg breaks and googlies, so that those people who took their lives in their hands and went down the wicket to him found that the ball was never there. He turned out to be an exceptional one-day bowler and was the major cause of our downfall in the two matches we lost to Pakistan.

As for his bowling in the Test series, that was something else again. He took 31 wickets in three matches – which is simply incredible. Yet for all our traumas, I found it a tremendous thrill to watch him bowl and actually bat against him. I'm sure the other batsmen did as well, although they were a bit horrified at the time.

It just goes to show what an impact top-class spin bowlers can make and why it is so important for us to produce them, which brings me back to the other two factors which have conspired against their development – limited-overs cricket and the way that captains treat young spinners.

Attitudes were rather different when Phillippe Edmonds and I first started to play for Middlesex in the early Seventies when the one-day game was only just beginning to take a hold. The Gillette Cup, later to become the NatWest Bank Trophy, had been launched in 1963, but the John Player League, now sponsored by Refuge Assurance, only started in 1969, and the Benson and Hedges Cup did not begin until 1972. It took a few more years after that for the full effect to be felt throughout the county game.

Now, with hindsight, I can see that it has affected the development of spin bowling to such an extent that I have every sympathy with youngsters trying to learn their craft and establish themselves in county cricket. The whole outlook has changed, so that it is not enough for them just to be able to spin the ball; they have to be capable of containing the batsmen – and of batting and fielding well, too. Instead of thinking about spin, spin, spin all the time – as we were able to do – they have to work very hard at every aspect of their game.

It is not easy for them, particularly when captains are intolerant of their shortcomings as bowlers. Young, inexperienced spinners cannot be expected to walk straight into county sides and get the upper hand of experienced batsmen who are looking to dominate them. They have to be nursed, encouraged, given confidence in their ability – and *not* be told brusquely that they aren't good enough and banished to the second team.

Don't get me wrong. I am not saying that they have to be wrapped in cotton wool; far from it. They have to learn the hard way, as I did. But I am not sure that they have either the opportunity or even the inclination to do that any more.

I was lucky to play most of my early games for Middlesex alongside Fred Titmus, because it undoubtedly helps the young spinner to be in the same side as someone as accomplished as he was. For a start, if you are getting smashed around, the captain can take you off and bring back the senior bowler who naturally commands a lot more respect from the batsmen.

It does make you feel inadequate at times because you are well aware that comparisons are being made. You also know that you are not going to get the chance to bowl at the most opportune moments because the object, after all, is always to win the game. Yet however frustrating that may be, you can learn an awful lot from watching an experienced spinner operate in those situations.

Youngsters rarely get the chance to do that nowadays. Nor do they seem to be getting the same kind of grooming in 2nd XI cricket as I had. Too often you find a bunch of inexperienced players with another inexperienced player as captain, and because he does not have the necessary authority they spend too much time messing around with the game instead of really getting down to it. They need senior players to bring them along and actually teach them how to be professional cricketers – and that applies to spin bowlers more than anybody.

There is so much for them to learn – which is why I believe that the time has come for county clubs to think more seriously about the way we are educating our cricketers and introduce development schemes of their own.

They should start at the grass roots, the very lowest level, because it alarms me to see how few youngsters are actually taking up the game. When I was a kid in South London, we used to play all the time on any patch of spare ground available, whether it was in the park or on the street. In some parts of the world, notably India and the West Indies, it is still much the same. But when you look around our inner cities you just do not see kids playing cricket any more – not even in areas where they have large Asian and West Indian communities.

The only explanation I can think of is that they are not getting the right kind of encouragement, and I think it is up to the county clubs and the professional cricketers themselves to give them that encouragement.

All the coaching I have ever done has been carried out overseas; and the same goes for most English players who spend their winters teaching young Australians, New Zealanders and South Africans how to become better cricketers. We are neglecting our own kids and we will pay dearly for that neglect in the future unless counties start providing facilities and setting up coaching camps where the most promising youngsters can learn how to play the game.

That kind of thing seems alien in this country, yet there is no reason why a county like Middlesex, for example, should not send out circulars to all the schools in their area saying that they are organizing a two-day camp, with senior players like myself in attendance to help and encourage youngsters to take up spin bowling. As long as enthusiastic people are involved, the kids themselves will be enthusiastic.

At a more advanced level, counties could also run coaching clinics where the best young players from local schools, as well as the club's own colts, could get together with the senior professionals for some expert tuition. It would not be feasible during the season itself because we play so much cricket that we want to spend any time off with our own families; but two afternoons a week could easily be set aside during pre-season training. It would also be an ideal opportunity for schoolteachers to go along with their pupils, watch what the professionals are doing and talk to them about different aspects of the game.

I am not forgetting the enterprise of Don Wilson, the MCC's chief coach, in setting up a 'school of excellence' at Lord's where 40 young players aged between 11 and 18 are being groomed as Test stars of the future. But we must start thinking about more wide-ranging schemes involving hundreds if not thousands of youngsters throughout the county – which should all be free. I was delighted to see that we were at least catching up with the Australians and New Zealanders in 1988 with the introduction of 'Kwik Cricket' – the English version of 'Kanga Cricket' and 'Kiwi Cricket' – which is a specially modified form of the game for primary schoolchildren, boys and girls. It was demonstrated during the Tests against the West Indies – and while it may not have had much effect on the outcome of the series, it is bound to pay dividends in the long term.

In the meantime, and from a purely selfish viewpoint, I

suppose I should not complain too bitterly about the desperate shortage of young and not-so-young spinners . . . since the way things were going there seemed little to prevent me from playing first-class cricket for several more years.

Fred Titmus was still playing regularly for Middlesex in 1976 when he was 43 – and not only playing but bowling 630 overs and taking 72 wickets – so I am certainly looking to play until I am 40. After that I would still like to carry on as long as I possibly can, although obviously that will depend on my fitness.

Touching wood, the back trouble I had at one stage of my career has not been a big problem in recent years, but I do feel that my legs are getting more tired and less willing to do the work. Considering the amount of cricket we play and all the travelling involved, I suppose that is only to be expected, and I am beginning to think that I have reached the age where all the exercising and running around we do before matches has become counter-productive.

I don't want any young cricketers to run away with the idea that physical fitness is not important, but it does get harder as you get older. You wake up in the morning thinking to yourself: 'Oh, no – I've got to get out of bed and start running around the ground.' That tends to take away some of your enthusiasm for what you really want to do – which is to get out there in the middle and play cricket.

Bernard Thomas started these rigorous training routines when he was England's physiotherapist, and they have since been taken up by all the Test-playing countries. But do cricketers really need them?

In the old days, they might have been a bit more overweight and a bit less athletic around the field, but their batting and bowling didn't seem to suffer too much. And, like that great old bowler Alec Bedser, I have become convinced that the best thing a bowler can do to prepare himself for bowling is to get into the nets and bowl.

So, as long as I can avoid stretching muscles that I don't need to stretch and aching in areas where I shouldn't ache, I hope to be able to carry on bowling whenever and wherever anyone wants me to bowl – with one reservation. I have no inclination to play in the West Indies again after my two tours there in 1981 and 1986.

It is not because of England's lack of success against them. It is not even because Viv Richards had a nasty habit of hitting me into the palm trees. It is solely because I did not enjoy playing there – and there is absolutely no point in playing if you don't enjoy it.

The Caribbean is a marvellous place for the tourist who wants no more than the sun, the sea and the sand, but it is not much fun for a spin bowler. And for all the problems England encounter on the subcontinent, I get far greater enjoyment out of visiting countries like India and Pakistan where the remarkable range of fast wickets, turning wickets and even flat wickets gives the cricket so much more variety and brings everybody into the game.

It is not like that in the West Indies, where the fast bowlers reign supreme. But one day, perhaps, things may be different – and I hope that this book will have had something to do with it.

Index

Index